Name

The Poor Souls' Friend

"Have pity on me, have pity on me, at least you my friends, because the hand of the Lord hath touched me."
—Job xix, 21.

MANUAL
OF THE
PURGATORIAN SOCIETY

CONTAINING SPIRITUAL READING AND
PRAYERS FOR EVERY DAY
OF THE MONTH
ALSO THE ORDINARY PRAYERS OF
A PIOUS CATHOLIC

Mother of Our Saviour, Pray for Us

Printed by:
MOS, Inc.
Mother of Our Savior Catholic Goods
PO Box 100 - Pekin, IN 47165
www.moscompany.com
800-451-3993

APPROBATION.

The little work "Manual of the Purgatorian Society" has for years been a source of spiritual help to the faithful, as well as a means of fostering devotion to the holy Souls in Purgatory. For that reason we hereby approve of its continued publication for the benefit especially of members of the Purgatorian Society.

MICHAEL A. GEARIN, C.SS.R.
Provincial.

Brooklyn, N. Y., June 20th, 1946.

Nihil Obstat:
JOHN M. A. FEARNS, S.T.D.,
Censor Librorum.

Imprimatur:
✠ FRANCIS CARDINAL SPELLMAN,
Archiepiscopus Neo-Eboracensis.
New York, July 28, 1946.

Copyright, 2006 - MOS, Inc.
Printed and Bound in the U.S.A.

ISBN: 0-9778570-2-6

PREFACE.

DEVOTION TO THE HOLY SOULS IN PURGATORY.

(*By St. Alphonsus Liguori.*)

"The practice of recommending to God the souls in Purgatory, that He may mitigate the great pains which they suffer, and that He may soon bring them to His glory, is most pleasing to the Lord and most profitable to us. For these blessed souls are His eternal spouses, and most grateful are they to those who obtain their deliverance from prison, or even a mitigation of their torments. When, therefore, they arrive in Heaven, they will be sure to remember all who have prayed for them. It is a pious belief that God manifests to them our prayers in their behalf, that they may also pray for us. It is true these blessed souls are not in a state to pray for themselves, because they are, so to speak, criminals atoning for their faults. However, because they are very dear to God, they can pray for us, and obtain for us the divine graces. St. Catherine of Bologna, when she wished to obtain any grace, had recourse to the souls in Purgatory, and her prayers were heard immediately. She declared that, by praying to those holy souls, she obtained many favors which she had sought through the intercession of the saints without obtaining them. The graces which devout persons are said to have received through these holy souls are innumerable.

But, if we wish for the aid of their prayers, it is just, it is even a duty, to relieve them by our suffrages. I say, *it is even a duty:* for Christian charity commands us to relieve our neighbors who stand in need of our assistance. But who among all our neighbors have so great need of our help as those holy prisoners? They are continually in that fire which torments more severely than any earthly fire. They are deprived of the sight of God, a torment far more excruciating than all other pains. Let us reflect that among these suffering souls are parents, or brothers, or relations and friends, who look to us for succor. Let us remember, moreover, that being in the condition of debtors for their sins, they cannot assist themselves. This thought should urge us forward to relieve them to the best of our ability. By assisting them we shall not only give great pleasure to God, but will acquire also great merit for ourselves. And, in return for our suffrages, these blessed souls will not neglect to obtain for us many graces from God, but particularly the grace of eternal life. I hold for certain that a soul delivered from Purgatory by the suffrages of a Christian, when she enters paradise, will not fail to say to God: "Lord, do not suffer to be lost that person who has liberated me from the prison of Purgatory, and has brought me to the enjoyment of Thy glory sooner than I had deserved."

The holy doctor then goes on to urge the faithful to do all in their power to relieve and liberate these blessed souls, by procuring Masses to be said for them, by alms, and by their own fervent prayers.

This little "Manual" will no doubt be welcomed by the members of the Purgatorian Society and other pious friends of the suffering souls in Purgatory.

Indulgenced Prayers to Aid the Suffering Souls.

NOTE: All the following indulgences are taken from the latest official book of indulgences—*Preces et Pia Opera*, Vatican Polyglot Press, 1938.

Indulgences attached to invocations and ejaculatory prayers can be gained by saying them merely *in one's mind*. (AAS. Vol. XXVI. p. 35).

A star (*) before a prayer signifies that if one says this prayer daily for a month he may gain a plenary indulgence, if, any time after completing the prescribed works he receives the Sacraments of Penance and Holy Communion, visits a church and there prays for the intention of the Holy Father.

When *Confession* and *Holy Communion* are prescribed for the gaining of an indulgence, those who are accustomed, unless lawfully hindered, to go to Confession at least *twice a month*, or to receive Holy Communion daily (though they may stay away one or two days during the week), may gain all indulgences, without actual confession, which would otherwise be necessary to gain them—except the indulgences of a jubilee. (Can. 931, Sec. 3.)

To pray for the *intention of the Holy Father* it is sufficient to recite *one* Our Father, Hail Mary, and Glory be to the Father.

To gain a plenary indulgence "Toties Quoties," *e. g.,* the *Portiuncula* or on *All Souls' Day,* for which a visit to the church is prescribed, you must say at least *six times* the Our Father, Hail Mary and Glory be to the Father for each visit. (Can. 934, Sec. 1, a b.)

To gain such an indulgence the *visits* may be made from noon of the preceding day till night of the specified day. (Can. 923.)

All the indulgences are *applicable* to the Souls in Purgatory. (Can. 930.)

FIRST DAY.
PRAYERS FOR THE HOLY SOULS.

One of the most consoling doctrines of the Catholic Church is that of the Communion of Saints. All men - the saints in Heaven, we upon earth, the souls in Purgatory — are members of one great family. By this "bond of perfection" which unites the Suffering and Triumphant Church with the Militant Church upon earth, incorporating them into one body, mutual charity becomes an obligation. This reciprocal love, being the duty of all men, renders it imperative that all should pray for one another, for in this general prayer, offered mutually, Christian charity is most beautifully and eloquently expressed.

From this general obligation we derive the special duty to pray for the suffering souls in Purgatory, who are unable in their extreme distress to do aught for their own relief. It has always been the belief of holy Church, that the faithful, united in the Communion of Saints, can mutually assist each other. As the saints in Heaven pray for us, so must we also offer our petitions for the suffering souls in Purgatory, that God in His goodness and mercy, may mitigate and shorten their punishment, and hasten their entrance into Heaven. It is the doctrine of the Church that the faithful upon earth are really able to relieve the temporal punishment of the holy souls in Purgatory. "In this," says the Roman Catechism, "the supreme mercy and goodness of God deserve our grateful acknowledgment and praise, that He has granted to our frailty the privilege that one may satisfy for another."

Prayer: O Lord, Jesus Christ, Thou Who hast said, "Where there are two or three gathered together in My name, there am I in the midst of them," (Matth. xviii. 20) look mercifully upon Thy holy Church, who implores Thy clemency in behalf of her suffering members. End their intense pain, and open unto them the portals of the heavenly Jerusalem, that they may praise and bless Thee forever and ever. Amen.

Special Intercession: Pray for those who, during the course of their earthly lives, did most to relieve the souls in Purgatory.

Eternal rest grant unto them, O Lord, and let perpetual light shine

upon them; may they rest in peace. Amen.

(300 days' indulgence each time. Say three times.) (No. 536)

Practice: Attend the public devotion for the suffering souls.

Invocation: My Jesus, mercy!

*(300 days' indulgence every time for the souls in Purgatory.) (No. 55)

SECOND DAY.
COMMEMORATION OF "ALL SOULS."

The commemoration of "All Souls" was instituted by the Church as a day of special prayer for all the faithful departed who are as yet deprived of the blissful contemplation of God, and the possession of Heaven. These holy souls endure most agonizing torments, and count the lingering moments of time, while awaiting release from prison, or, at least some relief in their intense pain. They have special confidence in their friends and relatives upon earth, hoping to be lovingly cherished in their memory, and aided by their fervent prayers. With holy Job they cry out: "Have pity on me, have pity on me, at least you, my friends, because the hand of the Lord hath touched me." (Job xix. 21.)

The anniversary of All Souls should serve to revive and confirm our devotion in behalf of the suffering souls in Purgatory, and induce us to make ample amends for our neglect of this duty during the year. "A gift hath grace in the sight of all the living, and restrain not grace from the dead." (Eccl. vii. 37.)

Prayer: O God, Creator and Redeemer of all the faithful, grant to the souls of Thy servants pardon of all their sins, that by pious supplications they may graciously obtain the remission they have always desired. Who livest and reignest world without end. Amen.

Special Intercession: Pray for the souls of those who suffer the greatest torments.

Eternal rest grant unto them, O Lord, and let perpetual light shine

upon them; may they rest in peace. Amen.

(Three times)

Practice: Examine how often, and in what manner you have practised prayer for the souls in Purgatory during the year.

Invocation: My Jesus, mercy!

THIRD DAY.

THE DOCTRINE OF PURGATORY.

The destiny awaiting us at death is not the same for all men: "He will render to every man according to his works." (Matth. xvi. 27.) Heaven, Hell, and Purgatory are the three places into which the souls of the departed are received. Heaven is the happy destination of perfectly pure and holy souls only; Hell the final doom of the reprobate; Purgatory, temporarily for the just, who are not as yet entirely purified. There God completes the punishment due to their faults, which were not sufficiently atoned for on earth; there He submits these holy souls to the last purgation, to cleanse them from the least stain, and, by fire, to bring them to that degree of perfected purity, which is necessary for them before being admitted to eternal bliss.

Hence there are two classes of souls in Purgatory: 1. Those who depart this life, stained by venial sins and imperfections.

2. Those who have repented sincerely of their mortal sins and confessed them, if possible, without having done sufficient penance for them. Judging from our lives, experience teaches us that most men deserve Purgatory for both causes.

Prayer: Graciously hear, O God, the fervent prayers we offer Thee for the suffering souls in Purgatory, who, not having satisfied Thy divine justice, confide in Thine infinite mercy and our intercessions. Extend unto them Thy consolations, and redeem them, through Christ, our Lord. Amen.

Special Intercession: Pray for the souls of those who suffer in Purgatory for little faults.

Eternal rest grant unto them, O Lord, and let perpetual light shine upon them; may they rest in peace. Amen.

(Three times.)

Practice: Be conscientious and faithful in the performance of little duties, and offer the inconvenience for the suffering souls.

Invocation: My Jesus, mercy!

FOURTH DAY.

EXPIATION FOR VENIAL SINS AND IMPERFECTIONS.

The judgments of God are very different from the judgments of men. "For: "My thoughts are not your thoughts; nor your ways My ways, saith the Lord. For as the heavens are exalted above the earth, so are My ways exalted above your ways, and My thoughts above your thoughts." (Is. lv. 8-9.) Though the judgments of God are severe, they are ever just. "Unto whomsoever much is given, of him much shall be required." (Luke xii. 48.) And St. Gregory the Great says: "Where grace has been augmented, there also the account has been increased." From those souls, upon whom God has bestowed great and special graces, He demands a more faithful cooperation, and the least infidelity to such grace is punished with extreme severity; the purgation or cleansing of these favored souls must be perfect in proportion to the high degree of glory to which they are to be exalted. In reference to prayer for the suffering souls, who are in Purgatory for venial sins and imperfections, we must observe that, though their time of suffering is comparatively short, and their punishment less vigorous, their pain and agony is more intense, owing to their yearning desire of perfect union with God. They are in utmost need of our fervent prayers, and will show their gratitude by their petitions for us before the throne of God, according to the speedy assistance we have given them during our earthly lives.

Prayer: Inflame within us, O Lord, the fire of Thy Divine love, that all our inordinate desires may be consumed here upon earth, thus rendering our prayers for the suffering souls in Purgatory more acceptable to Thee and beneficial to them. Through Christ, our Lord. Amen.

Special Intercession: Pray for the souls who are nearest their deliverance.

Eternal rest grant unto them, O Lord, and let perpetual light shine

upon them; may they rest in peace. Amen.

(Three times)

Practice: Mortify your prevailing weakness or inclination.

Invocation: My Jesus, mercy!

FIFTH DAY.

THE SUFFERINGS OF PURGATORY.

The sufferings of Purgatory are twofold: the pain of loss, and the torture of the senses; both in proportion to temporal punishment unremitted. Having committed sin, the soul has turned away from God, thus increasing the pain of loss, or, according to our ideas, God departs from that soul and deprives her of His beatific vision. By sin, the soul has been attached to creatures, making improper use of them, displeasing to God, hence the severe punishment, consisting in the pain of the sense. God permits that those who have abandoned their Creator, and bestowed their affections upon creatures, are chastised by the same, for we read in the Book of Wisdom: "By what things a man sinneth, by the same also is he tormented." (Wis. xi. 17.)

God has not revealed, nor has the Church ever taught in what manner or to what extent the souls in Purgatory suffer, but it is the opinion of the holy Fathers and Doctors of the Church that, what St. Paul writes to the Corinthians, (1, iii. 15) "But he himself shall be saved: yet so as by fire," must be taken in a literal sense, which is accepted also by St. Thomas Aquinas.

Prayer: O Lord, by Thine infinite love and clemency, graciously grant to the suffering souls in Purgatory remittance of their punishment. Receive them into Thy eternal glory, that blessed by Thy beatific vision, they may praise and adore Thee for ever and ever. Amen.

Special Intercession: Pray for the souls of those who have suffered for the longest time in Purgatory.

Eternal rest grant unto them, O Lord, and let perpetual light shine upon them; may they rest in peace. Amen.

(Three times)

Practice: Do not let human respect prevent you from performing a duty.

Invocation: My Jesus, mercy!

SIXTH DAY.
THE PAIN OF LOSS.

The spiritual suffering, or the pain of loss, is the greatest pain of Purgatory, according to the Fathers of the Church. No one can comprehend the great suffering of a soul departed, which, in all its ardent desire for the highest and only good, sees itself ever repulsed as an object of God's avenging justice.

St. Alphonsus writes: "Far greater than the pain of sense in Purgatory is that pain which the holy souls must endure in being deprived of the vision of God. Because these souls are inflamed, not only with a natural, but with a supernatural love of God, they are so vehemently attracted to the union with their highest good, that, in being repulsed through their own fault, they experience so violent a pain as would kill them instantly if death were possible to them." Therefore, says St. Chrysostom, "this pain of being deprived of God is a far greater pain for them than the pain of the senses. The fire of hell increased a thousand times would not cause them such great suffering as does this pain of the loss of God."

Prayer: O God, Father of mercies, grant the ardent desire of the souls in

Purgatory who yearn to behold Thee. Send down to them Thy holy angel with the joyful tidings that the moment of their redemption has come, that their exile is ended, and bless them by the perfect union with Thee forever. Through Christ, our Lord. Amen.

Special Intercession: Pray for the souls who are punished for their forgetfulness of the holy Presence of God during their lives.

Eternal rest grant unto them, O Lord, and let perpetual light shine upon them; may they rest in peace. Amen.

(Three times)

Practice: Try to remember at all times the holy Presence of God.

Invocation: My Jesus, mercy!

SEVENTH DAY.
PAIN OF SORROW FOR SIN.

The soul departed, before the judgment-seat of God, is enlightened with a perfect knowledge of the purity and sanctity of her Divine Judge, clearly perceiving the stains with which she is sullied, and her extreme unworthiness of union with God. The thought: I have offended God, Who is everlasting beauty and perfection; I am not yet worthy to appear before the face of the Lord, Who is infinitely holy, not worthy to take possession of my dwelling-place in Heaven, - is the greatest sorrow of the suffering soul. Much more clearly than during their earthly lives do these holy souls comprehend the perfections of God, and love Him above all things; therefore the thought of having offended Him is a piercing sorrow which surpasses all their other sufferings.

St. Ambrose tells us, there is no greater agony than remorse of conscience caused by sin. There are examples on record, of men who died from the effects of this vehement sorrow. Yet, how much more intense must be the contrition of the suffering souls, who fully understand the great malice of sin! We know by our own experience that the depth of sorrow for having offended a person is equal to the love we bear him. The holy souls in Purgatory, being inflamed with a perfect love of God, their perfect contrition for sin is their greatest sorrow.

Prayer: O God, Father of grace and mercy! graciously regard the deep sorrow of the suffering souls in Purgatory. Deign to accept their love, and grant them remission of their punishment, that, united with Thee, they may praise Thy goodness forever. Through Christ, our Lord. Amen.

Special Intercession: Pray for the souls who, while on earth, loved God most ardently.

Eternal rest grant unto them, O Lord, and let perpetual light shine upon them; may they rest in peace. Amen. (Three times)

Practice: Try to make an act of perfect contrition for your sins.

Invocation: My Jesus, mercy!

EIGHTH DAY.
PAIN OF HELPLESSNESS AND DESOLATION.

The souls in Purgatory have entered into the realm of Divine Justice. The penance and satisfaction due for their faults must be made, either by the pain of Purgatory itself, or by the suffrages of the faithful, consisting in prayer, good works, and the spiritual treasure of indulgences bestowed upon them; for the suffering souls can no longer merit, and are entirely unable to assist themselves. A sick man and a beggar have a tongue to ask for help, and the very sight of their misery will move others to compassion. The suffering souls, however, have no resource but that of patience, resignation, and hope. To all their moans there is but one answer, "the night hath come, in which no man can work."

Hence in their extreme desolation and distress, they incessantly cry out to us for relief and assistance; but since they cannot do this in a manner perceptible to us, holy Church does it for them, by instituting many touching devotions in their behalf. Can we, then, be cold and heartless towards these souls?—"A hard heart will fare evil at the last." Be not then indifferent to your own interests.

Prayer: Have mercy, O Lord, upon the suffering souls in Purgatory, in their helplessness and desolation. Comfort them by the prayers and petitions of the angels and the just in Heaven and upon earth; shorten the time of their suffering, and reward them with joys eternal. Through Christ, our Lord. Amen.

Special Intercession: Pray for the most forsaken and helpless souls.

Eternal rest grant unto them, O Lord, and let perpetual light shine upon them; may they rest in peace. Amen.

(Three times)

Practice: Deny yourself a little comfort, or some special consolation, and offer it for the most forsaken souls in Purgatory.

Invocation: My Jesus, mercy!

NINTH DAY.
PAIN OF FIRE IN PURGATORY.

The Church has given no decision regarding the word "fire" in relation to Purgatory; but according to Theologians and Doctors of the Church, we are to understand a material fire. Concerning this, Bishop Colmar of Mayence, a great friend of the holy souls, writes: "Besides being deprived of the vision of God, the souls in Purgatory must also endure the tortures of a fire, the effects of which are so much more painful, as it is an instrument in the avenging hand of God; a fire, as St. Augustine says, in comparison to which our material fire is as nothing; a fire that entirely penetrates the soul, in whatever manner this may be accomplished.

How, and to what extent this is done, we know not, but may draw our conclusion from similar instances.— "In like manner," says St. Gregory the Great, "as the fallen angels, although pure spirits, are tormented by the material fire of hell, so may a similar fire torture the souls of the departed in Purgatory." The justice of God can punish a spirit by means of a material substance, as well as He can, in His omnipotence, give life to a body by the agency of a spirit. According to the holy Fathers, the fire of Purgatory does not differ from the fire of hell, excepting in point of duration. "It is the same fire," says St. Thomas, "that torments the reprobate in hell, and the just in Purgatory. The least pain in Purgatory," he adds, "surpasses the greatest sufferings of this life." Nothing but eternal duration makes the fire of hell more terrible than that of Purgatory.

Prayer: Refresh, O Lord, the suffering souls in Purgatory, with the dew of Thy grace, that their pains may be relieved, and, in Thy mercy, hasten the moment of their deliverance, that they may meet Thee in Heaven, where no fire but that of Thy holy love shall consume them. Through Christ our Lord. Amen.

Special Intercession: Pray for all the souls in Purgatory, particularly for those who are forgotten by their relatives.

Eternal rest grant unto them, O Lord, and let perpetual light shine

upon them; may they rest in peace. Amen. (Three times)

Practice: Endeavor to spread the devotion for the holy souls in Purgatory as much as possible.

Invocation: My Jesus, mercy!

TENTH DAY.
THE DURATION OF PURGATORY.

Concerning the duration of Purgatory, the Church simply tells us that it is not a place of eternal pain, but will end at the last judgment; neither are we informed of the length of time required for the purification of a soul. According to St. Thomas Aquinas, the soul, to be reunited to her Creator in Heaven, must be in the state of primitive innocence which adorned her when she proceeded from His hand. The image of God must be entirely restored within her, commensurate to the degree of glory awaiting her in Heaven.

From this it is evident that the suffering souls cannot enter Heaven until perfectly cleansed, either by their pains or by the suffrages of the faithful. With the royal Prophet they cry out in plaintive voice: "As the hart panteth after the fountains of water, so my soul panteth after Thee, O God! When shall I come and appear before the face of God?" (Ps. xli. 2-3.) They suffer until entirely purified, until the last farthing of their debt is discharged. Increased and intensified pain will probably supply the want of time for the souls who shall not have rendered full satisfaction by the last day of universal judgment.

Prayer: O God, the Dispenser of pardon, and Friend of human salvation, we implore Thee, by the intercession of the Blessed Virgin Mary, and all Thy saints, grant to the souls of our brethren, relatives, benefactors, and all the faithful departed, the joys of eternal bliss. Through Christ, our Lord. Amen.

Special Intercession: Pray for the souls who are most desirous of obtaining help from you.

Eternal rest grant unto them, O Lord, and let perpetual light shine upon them; may they rest in peace. Amen.

(Three times)

Practice: Mortify your curiosity.

Invocation: My Jesus, mercy!

ELEVENTH DAY.
OUR DUTY TO RELIEVE THE SOULS IN PURGATORY.

In bestowing charity upon any person, we are usually guided by the degree of his poverty; but, who is in such great need as he who possesses absolutely nothing, owes a heavy debt, is unable to labor or gain any merit, or even to beg, and must nevertheless suffer the most excruciating torments until the last farthing has been paid? There is a universal law to assist the needy, which extends even to strangers; but here the obligation is greatest, because among these souls in Purgatory, are such as were intimately connected with us, who suffer, perhaps, for having loved us excessively. Among the sufferers are our fathers, mothers, brothers, sisters, relatives, and friends. How exceedingly painful for them to be forgotten and deserted even by those whose happiness they promoted during their sojourn upon earth; to see the possessions left to their children foolishly squandered, they themselves not receiving the benefit of the least farthing thereof! What proofs of extreme coldness and ingratitude! Were any of these persons afflicted with the least pain upon earth, we would do all in our power to relieve them, but, as it is, we are devoid of all sympathy, and leave them in their terrible suffering and anguish.

Prayer: Have mercy, O Lord, upon the suffering souls in Purgatory, and mitigate the severity of Thy judgment, that they, who, during their earthly lives believed in Thee, hoped in Thee, and loved Thee, may receive the crown of justice in Heaven. Through Christ, our Lord. Amen.

Special Intercession: Pray for the souls of those who are suffering for their negligence in praying for the souls in Purgatory.

Eternal rest grant unto them, O Lord, and let perpetual light shine upon them; may they rest in peace. Amen.

(Three times)

Practice: Suffer patiently the disagreeable occurrences in your intercourse with others.

Invocation: My Jesus, mercy!

TWELFTH DAY.

GRAND DISPLAY IS OF NO VALUE TO THE HOLY SOULS.

In regard to pompous displays for the departed, St. Augustine says: "Costly funerals and expensive displays may afford the living some consolation, but are of no benefit to the departed." He adds, however, "Let care be bestowed upon funerals and the erection of monuments; for Holy Writ reckons these among good works. Let all perform these last services for their departed, and thereby relieve their own sorrow; but let them show greater zeal, care, and generosity in succoring the souls of the departed by Masses, prayers, and alms, and thus give evidence not only of a temporal, but also a spiritual love for those who are departed in body only, but not in spirit. According to a rule of the Church, flowers should be used at funerals of children only;

circumstances may at times justify a deviation from this rule, but, at all events, it is unpardonable if the expense connected with this display deprives the soul departed of any spiritual assistance.

Prayer: We beseech Thee, O Lord, by Thy infinite mercy, do not despise our prayers in behalf of the souls in Purgatory, but grant them the peace and consolation we desire for them. Through Christ, our Lord. Amen.

Special Intercession: Pray for the souls of those who were remembered by a pompous funeral only, and have no relief in their pain.

Eternal rest grant unto them, O Lord, and let perpetual light shine upon them; may they rest in peace. Amen. (Three times)

Practice: Accompany the funeral of a poor person, at the first opportunity.

Invocation: My Jesus, mercy!

THIRTEENTH DAY.

THE SPECIAL DUTY OF EVERY ONE TO AID THE FAITHFUL DEPARTED.

Besides the general duty imposed upon us by the divine law of charity, there is a special obligation incumbent upon every one to assist particular souls. This duty devolves upon us in consequence of the personal relations with such souls during their earthly career; for, whatever be the condition of man in life, he will have among the souls, departed, who may be suffering in Purgatory, some to whom he is indebted for particular favors and benefits.

But what could more forcibly elicit our charity and gratitude than to behold our loved ones and our benefactors in extreme distress, while we have the means of alleviating their suffering! That person does not possess a spark of Christian charity, who, from neglect or indolence, suffers the souls of his friends to be tormented in the flames of Purgatory.

Prayer: Revive, O Lord, within the hearts of Thy faithful, an active commiseration for the brethren gone before us, that they may not, by our indifference or neglect, suffer without relief and assistance. Through Christ, our Lord. Amen.

Special Intercession: Pray for the souls of those who are neglected by their relatives and friends.

Eternal rest grant unto them, O Lord, and let perpetual light shine upon them; may they rest in peace. Amen.

(Three times)

Practice: Bestow alms for the relief of the suffering souls.

Invocation: My Jesus, mercy!

FOURTEENTH DAY.

SPECIAL DUTY OF CHILDREN TOWARDS THEIR DECEASED PARENTS.

"Honor thy father, and forget not the groanings of thy mother. Remember that thou hadst not been born but through them, and make a return to them: as they have done for thee." (Eccl. vii. 29-30.) Next to God, our parents are our greatest benefactors, entitled to most tender love and gratitude, which is the sacred duty of every child. This duty does not end with this life; it is extended even to eternity. Should our departed parents find no relief in their pains? Must they cry out in bitter anguish: "I have reared sons and daughters, but they have forgotten me?"

If we compassionate the misery of strangers, if we do not heartlessly send a beggar from our doors, oh, let us remember how near and dear father and mother are to us, and how greatly we are indebted to them. After their death we owe them prayers, alms, good works, and Masses. They cry out to us for mercy. Would it not be the highest degree of ingratitude were we to forget those who bestowed their best love and care upon us in life? The commandment of God, "Honor thy father and thy mother," is an obligation also towards our deceased parents.

Prayer: O God, Who hast commanded us to honor father and mother, look in loving kindness upon the souls of my father and mother, and forgive them their trespasses, and grant unto me the joy of being reunited to them in the glorious light of everlasting life. Through Jesus Christ, Thy Son, our Lord. Amen.

Special Intercession: Pray for the souls of parents who have been forgotten by their children.

Eternal rest grant unto them, O Lord, and let perpetual light shine upon them; may they rest in peace. Amen. (Three times)

Practice: Mortify yourself by an act of obedience.

Invocation: My Jesus, mercy!

FIFTEENTH DAY.
WE SHOULD BE IN THE STATE OF GRACE WHEN GAINING INDULGENCES FOR THE POOR SOULS.

Holy Church teaches us that the state of grace is necessary to perform works that are merit-bearing for ourselves, and many Saints and holy teachers of the science of God apply this same teaching to works and prayers which have indulgences attached to them and are to be applied to the Poor Souls. It is certain that if confession and Holy Communion are demanded for gaining the particular indulgence, the indulgence is not gained unless the person who performs these works is in God's favor at the time. A person who may be, unfortunately, in the state of mortal sin, can have Masses said for the faithful departed. He himself will acquire no merit thereby, but the suffering souls will derive the full benefit of the Holy Sacrifice. As we should always strive to be in the friendship and grace of God, if we have any doubt about our condition or are certain that we have lost God's favor then before trying to gain an indulgence let us confess our sins or at least strive to make an act of perfect contrition.

"He that abideth in Me," says Christ, "and I in him, the same beareth much fruit, for without Me you can do nothing." (John xv, 5) If, then, we are incapable of gaining merit for ourselves, how can we expect to benefit others? St. Francis Xavier says: "Before being intent upon delivering souls from Purgatory, take heed to redeem your own souls from hell;" and here we may add the word of the Lord spoken by His prophet: "Wash yourselves, be clean, take away the evil of your devices from my eyes: cease to do perversely." (Isaias i. 16.)

Prayer: Grant us the grace, O Lord! to avoid sin at all times, and confirm us in Thy charity, that, by Thy bounty, our supplications for the suffering souls may be acceptable to Thee, and beneficial to them. Through Christ, our Lord: Amen.

Special Intercession: Pray for the souls of those who were careful never to lose the grace of God.

Eternal rest grant unto them, O Lord, and let perpetual light shine upon them; may they rest in peace. Amen. (Three times)

Practice: Make an act of perfect contrition.

Invocation: My Jesus, mercy!

SIXTEENTH DAY.
THE EFFICACY OF PRAYER FOR THE SUFFERING SOULS.

"It is a holy and wholesome thought to pray for the dead that they may be loosed from their sins." (2 Mach. xii. 46)

Prayer for the dead is *holy*, because

pleasing to God; *wholesome,* because, through the merciful goodness of God it accomplishes its sublime and charitable object. Nothing is so pleasing to God as the sacrifice of love and mercy, especially when offered for the suffering souls, whom He loves most tenderly, because they are holy and sure of Heaven.

To relieve the suffering souls we can do scarcely anything more salutary than to gain indulgences applicable to them, offering to God the perfect satisfaction of Christ and the saints, and performing good works in their behalf, that they may be comforted or entirely delivered from the pains of Purgatory.

A suffering soul may receive an entire or a temporary remission of her penalty, in accordance with the indulgence applied, being either plenary or partial.

Prayer: Open, O Lord! the rich treasures of Thy holy Church, in favor of the souls in Purgatory that they may receive full pardon, or, at least some relief in their pains; and grant us grace to deliver and to comfort a great number of suffering souls by prayer and good works. Through Christ, our Lord. Amen.

Special Intercession: Pray for the souls, who, during their earthly career, endeavored to gain many indulgences for the faithful departed.

Eternal rest grant unto them, O Lord, and let perpetual light shine upon them; may they rest in peace. Amen. (Three times)

Practice: Apply all the indulgences you can gain to the souls in Purgatory.

Invocation: My Jesus, mercy!

SEVENTEENTH DAY.
THE MANNER IN WHICH THE CHURCH BESTOWS INDULGENCES UPON THE SOULS IN PURGATORY.

The Church does not apply indulgences to the souls in Purgatory, as she does to the faithful upon earth, by the tribunal of penance and absolution, but confers them simply by pious supplications and sacrifices offered in their behalf; thus they are relieved indirectly. The Holy Church opens her rich treasures of merit and satisfaction in proportion to the suffrages of the faithful, offering expiation and fervent prayers to God for the relief of the suffering souls, according to the value of the indulgences gained in their behalf.

God has reserved to Himself the right to accept entirely, or in part, the satisfaction offered for any soul in Purgatory. This acceptance depends upon His holy and adorable Will, and, perhaps, in great measure upon the care of the soul to render herself worthy of the Divine assistance during her earthly career. Besides, there may be some obligations neglected by the person who intends to gain the indulgence, owing to ignorance or forgetfulness on his part. Therefore, we have no assurance whatever that an indulgence given by us to the holy souls has had the desired effect. Considering this, we should prepare most carefully, and fulfill all obligations required for gaining an indulgence. However, let us place, with entire confidence, the application of indulgences to departed souls especially dear to us, into the tender hand of Divine mercy.

Prayer: Have mercy, O Lord, upon the suffering souls in Purgatory, mitigate the severity of Thy judgments; let the infinite merits of Thine only-begotten Son, and those of Thy saints, assist the holy souls, and deliver them from their sufferings. Through Christ, our Lord. Amen.

Special Intercession: Pray for the souls of those who neglected to gain indulgences for the souls in Purgatory.

Eternal rest grant unto them, O Lord, and let perpetual light shine

upon them; may they rest in peace. Amen. (Three times)

Practice: Offer all indulgences you may gain to-day, for the souls in Purgatory.

Invocation: My Jesus, mercy!

EIGHTEENTH DAY.
THE EFFICACY OF HOLY MASS FOR THE DEPARTED.

The Sacrifice of the Mass is the great devotion of the Catholic Church, and, of all means to assist the souls in Purgatory, none is more valuable or meritorious; for there Jesus Christ offers Himself and His infinite merits to His Heavenly Father, by the hands of the Priest, in behalf of the suffering souls. The unbloody Sacrifice of the Mass does not essentially differ from the sacrifice of the cross, but only accidentally as to the mode of oblation, and no limit can be placed to the effect of this great sacrifice, which contains in itself all graces.

From this inestimable efficacy, however, we may not infer that the offering of one Mass is sufficient to release the souls we love; for, though the Sacrifice on Calvary was infinite, we cannot conclude that the *application* of it, through the Mass, must also be infinite. St. Thomas Aquinas tells us, it was not the intention of Jesus Christ to bestow the full efficacy of His suffering and death, which is celebrated in every Mass, upon us; His merits are applied according to His Adorable Will, for the ways of God are often inscrutable.

It is very salutary, therefore, to have the Holy Sacrifice offered frequently for the repose of a soul. Should the souls who are dear to us, for whom we intercede in this manner, be already in the enjoyment of eternal bliss, Divine wisdom and goodness will bestow the merit of the Masses offered on other suffering souls.

Prayer: O Lord, Jesus Christ: Who didst institute the unbloody Sacrifice of the Mass in commemoration of Thy Sacrifice upon the cross, we beseech Thee, bestow the merits of this Holy Sacrifice upon the souls in Purgatory, that they may soon be released from their pains. Who livest and reignest, world without end. Amen.

Special Intercession: Pray for the souls of those who were most zealous to assist at Mass.

Eternal rest grant unto them, O Lord, and let perpetual light shine upon them; may they rest in peace. Amen.

(Three times)

Practice: Assist at Mass for the relief of the suffering souls.

Invocation: My Jesus, mercy!

NINETEENTH DAY.

HOLY COMMUNION OF GREAT BENEFIT TO THE DEPARTED.

The holy Doctor and Cardinal, St. Bonaventure, of the Order of St. Francis, who wrote much concerning the holy souls, urges especially frequent communion in their behalf. "Let the love and compassion for your neighbor," so he writes, "lead you to the holy table; for nothing is so well calculated to obtain eternal rest for the holy souls." This is confirmed by the following example: Louis Blosius relates that a pious servant of God, in a vision, beheld a departed friend, wrapped in flames, and learned from him that he suffered terribly, because he had received our Lord in Holy Communion with but little preparation. "Therefore," added this departed friend, "I beg of you, for the love we bore each other, to communicate for the benefit of my soul, but to do so with great preparation and fervor; I then hope certainly to be released from the terrible sufferings that I have indeed well deserved for my negligence towards the Blessed Sacrament." The friend at once complied with the request, and having received Holy Communion with due preparation, he saw the same soul enveloped in light, winging its happy flight to Heaven, to behold face to face the King of eternal glory.

Prayer: O Lord, Jesus Christ, Who in the Most Holy Sacrament of the Altar hast given us Thine own flesh and blood for the nourishment of our souls, and a pledge of our own future resurrection, grant us the grace always to receive worthily this Most Holy Mystery, that it may be to us and the souls in Purgatory a source of salvation. Who livest and reignest, world without end. Amen.

Special Intercession: Pray for the

souls who were negligent in their preparation for Holy Communion.

Eternal rest grant unto them, O Lord, and let perpetual light shine upon them; may they rest in peace. Amen. (Three times)

Invocation: My Jesus, mercy!

TWENTIETH DAY.
LOVE OF THE BLESSED VIRGIN TOWARDS THE SOULS IN PURGATORY.

Since our Divine Redeemer has given us Mary as a mother, when, dying upon the cross, He spoke to His disciple, "Behold thy mother," the Blessed Virgin regards us all as her beloved children, but she harbors most tender feelings of maternal love towards the suffering souls in Purgatory. Let us then afford the Mother of love the satisfaction of giving abundant suffrages to the souls in Purgatory. Taking into consideration the great prerogatives of the Blessed Virgin, and the infinite love of the Holy Trinity towards her, we cannot doubt that by her merit and intercession every penitent suffering soul would be delivered, that Purgatory could be emptied at once, were such according to the inscrutable ways of God.

But God has His own designs, founded on His infinite wisdom, justice, and mercy. The Blessed Virgin does not pray to have all the suffering souls delivered at once, for her will is in perfect conformity to the Will of God, and she exercises her dominion over the souls in Purgatory in perfect union with this Divine Will.

St. Bernardine of Siena applies to Mary the text of Holy Writ, "I have walked in the waves of the sea," (Eccl. xxiv. 8.) and adds, "She descends into that sea of fire, quenching the flames for the suffering souls."

Denys the Carthusian attests that the souls in Purgatory experience the same joy and relief, at the mere mention of her name, that consoling words bring to the bedridden sick.

Prayer: O most holy and glorious Virgin Mary, Blessed Mother of our Lord! we place our petitions for the suffering souls into thy hands; cleanse them from all imperfections, and, by thy intercession, obtain for them eternal rest. Through the same Jesus Christ, Thy Son, our Lord. Amen.

Special Intercession: Pray for the souls who were most zealous in their devotion to the Blessed Virgin.

Eternal rest grant unto them, O Lord, and let perpetual light shine upon them; may they rest in peace. Amen. (Three times)

Practice: Say the Litany of the Blessed Virgin for the suffering souls.

Invocation: My Jesus, mercy!

TWENTY-FIRST DAY.

EFFICACY OF THE ROSARY FOR THE SUFFERING SOULS.

St. Dominic declares that the redemption of the holy souls from Purgatory is one of the principal effects of the Rosary. The Venerable Alanus writes that many of the brethren had appeared to them whilst reciting the Rosary, and had declared that next to the Holy Sacrifice of the Mass there was no more powerful means than the Rosary to help the suffering souls. Also, that numerous souls were daily released thereby, who otherwise would have been obliged to remain there for years. St. Alphonsus Liguori therefore says: "If we wish to be of material assistance to the souls in Purgatory, we must always recommend them in our prayers to the Blessed

Virgin Mary, and especially offer the holy Rosary for them."

Let us then frequently and with devotion recite the Rosary, which is so pleasing to our blessed Mother, recommended most especially by the Holy Church, discloses to us a rich source of grace, and is so efficacious in relieving the suffering souls and opening Heaven to them. Should our labor prevent us from reciting the entire Rosary every day, let us, at least, say it in part. This simple homage to the Queen of Heaven will draw down great blessings upon us, and the holy souls will be wonderfully consoled and relieved, if this devotion be offered in their behalf.

Prayer: Graciously hear, O Lord! the prayer we offer Thee in the holy Rosary, in honor of Mary, Thy Virgin Mother, for the relief of the souls in Purgatory, while by devoutly meditating upon Thy holy life and suffering, we implore Thy divine assistance.

Who livest and reignest, world without end. Amen.

Special Intercession: Pray for the souls who were most devoted to the holy Rosary.

Eternal rest grant unto them, O Lord, and let perpetual light shine upon them; may they rest in peace. Amen. (Three times)

Practice: Recite the Rosary for the suffering souls.

Invocation: My Jesus, mercy!

TWENTY-SECOND DAY.
ALMS-GIVING AFFORDS GREAT RELIEF TO THE DEPARTED.

Besides prayer and other acts of devotion, there are practical good works we can perform for the relief of the suffering souls, among which alms-giving is one of the most prominent; for this, being a work of mercy, is especially efficacious in obtaining mercy for the holy souls. Not the rich alone are able to give alms; the poor can do so as well; since it is not the value of the gift, but the good intention, in which it is bestowed, that is acceptable in the sight of God. We also shall, one day, be numbered among the suffering souls, and who is in greater need and poverty than they? The most miserable beggar in this world can at least complain of his wants, and ask others to assist him; but the souls in Purgatory cannot do even this, for, the instances in which they are permitted to implore aid of the living are exceptional cases, and very few are on record. What consolation it will afford us when, in our own great time of need, the poor whom we befriended and comforted upon earth, in the company of the holy souls, whom we delivered by offering this work of mercy for them, shall come to our assistance by their prayers and pious supplications! Therefore, says Holy Scripture: "Do good to thy friend before thou die; and according to thy ability, stretching out thy hand, give to the poor." (Eccl. xiv. 13.)

Prayer: Lord! graciously look down upon the alms we offer for the redemption of the captive souls in Purgatory. Bestow upon them the full merit thereof, that they may be able to discharge their debt; accept, we beseech Thee, this boon of charity, that delivered from debt and penalty, Thou mayest lead them into Thy heavenly kingdom. Through Christ, our Lord. Amen.

Special Intercession: Pray for the souls of those who upon earth gave alms for the relief of the suffering souls.

Eternal rest grant unto them, O Lord, and let perpetual light shine upon them; may they rest in peace. Amen. (Three times)

Practice: Bestow a gift upon a poor

person, and offer the merit for the souls in Purgatory.

Invocation: My Jesus, mercy!

TWENTY-THIRD DAY.

WORKS OF PENANCE FOR THE HOLY SOULS.

The Church has at all times recommended, and the saints have always had recourse to works of penance as the best means of obtaining extraordinary graces from God, and there is no doubt that these works of mortification have great efficacy for the departed. Although great works of penance and mortification are not expected of every one, yet there is no one who could not occasionally deny himself a part of some favorite dish or some amusement, mortify his eyes, ears, or tongue, observe silence for a short time, bear in patience the pain of sickness, heat or cold, or any other adversity, or curb his self-will and evil inclinations; in fact, bear with submission and gratitude to God everything that causes pain or distress.

Such charity lovingly bestowed on the holy souls of our dear departed will call down rich blessings upon us, and obtain for us strength to endure our own sufferings.

"Know ye that the Lord will hear your prayers if you continue with perseverance in fastings and prayers, in the sight of the Lord." (Judith iv. 11.)

Prayer: Grant us, O Lord! the grace to walk before Thee in penance and mortification, and in these works to remember the souls in Purgatory. Deign to accept what we in the spirit of charity offer for the comfort and relief of these penitent souls. Through Christ, our Lord. Amen.

Special Intercession: Pray for the

souls of those who bestowed the merit of their mortifications upon the holy souls.

Eternal rest grant unto them, O Lord, and let perpetual light shine upon them; may they rest in peace. Amen. (Three times)

Practice: Perform an act of mortification for the souls in Purgatory.

Invocation: My Jesus, mercy!

TWENTY-FOURTH DAY.
VALUE OF GOOD WORKS OFFERED FOR THE SUFFERING SOULS.

St. Thomas Aquinas, the Angelic Doctor, affirms that the succor and suffrage given to the departed are more acceptable to God than that which is bestowed upon the living, because the former are more in need and unable to obtain help for themselves as the living can. The revered Louis

Blosius, a great master of the spiritual life, says: "Our good and merciful Lord loves the souls of His elect, who must be purified after death, and desires their release so ardently, that whenever in Christian charity we set free, by our suffrages, any soul from Purgatory, we do a thing as acceptable to God as if we had delivered the Lord Himself from a hard captivity. He promises to give us as full a recompense as such a work of mercy practised towards Himself would deserve; for He Himself has said: "Amen, I say to you: as long as you did it to one of these, My least brethren, you did it to Me." (Matth. xxv. 40.)

The same is affirmed by St. Ambrose: "Whatever we do for the suffering souls, with a pious intention, will revert to our own merit, and will be returned a hundred fold, at the hour of death."

Prayer: O God of love and mercy!

animated with charity and compassion for our departed brothers and sisters, we offer Thee our prayers and good works, and supplicate Thee to accept them as a propitiatory sacrifice in their behalf. Through Christ, our Lord. Amen.

Special Intercession: Pray for the souls of those who were negligent in offering good works for the suffering souls.

Eternal rest grant unto them, O Lord, and let perpetual light shine upon them; may they rest in peace. Amen. (Three times)

Practice: Bear your sufferings with patience, and offer them for the holy souls.

Invocation: My Jesus, mercy!

TWENTY-FIFTH DAY.
GRATITUDE OF THE HOLY SOULS.

The prayers and works of charity which we bestow on the suffering souls in Purgatory, not only increase our spiritual merit, they also call forth the gratitude of the holy, ransomed souls; for when these dear souls are, by our endeavors, admitted to the vision of God, they cease not to prove the warmth of their thankfulness and love by imploring for us the help of which we are so much in need in the manifold dangers and great troubles of life. How can the faithful departed, who are loved by God so tenderly, and predestined to glory, fail to be able to pray, not, indeed, for themselves, because they are not in a condition to merit, yet to pray with efficacy for their benefactors still alive?

Not only will they speedily pay their debt of gratitude to those who befriend them, but, our dear Lord Himself, Whose greater honor and glory we have promoted by our devotion to the holy souls, will readily assist them to requite the services rendered them by the faithful upon earth. St. Alphonsus Liguori says: "He who assists these distressed souls, so tenderly loved by God, may confidently hope for his salvation; for, when such a soul obtains deliverance through his prayers and good works, it incessantly prays for his salvation, and God will deny nothing to such a soul."

Prayer: We beseech Thee, O Lord! vouchsafe to hear the suffering souls, who supplicate Thee for their benefactors, that we, in union with these holy souls, for whom we offer fervent prayers upon earth, may praise Thy mercies forever. Through Christ, our Lord. Amen.

Special Intercession: Pray for the souls who suffer for their faults against charity.

Eternal rest grant unto them, O Lord, and let perpetual light shine upon them; may they rest in peace. Amen. (Three times)

Practice: Bestow charity upon

others without expecting gratitude. *Invocation:* My Jesus, mercy!

TWENTY-SIXTH DAY.
BY DELIVERING THE SOULS FROM PURGATORY WE PROMOTE THE HONOR OF GOD.

According to St. Paul, the Apostle, the honor and glory of God should be the principal motive of all our actions: "Whether you eat or drink, or whatsoever else you do; do all things for the glory of God" (1. Cor. x. 31.) "The glorification of God" ought to be our special aim in our works, most particularly in our acts of charity for the dead; and justly so, for, by delivering these holy souls, we lead them to Heaven, where alone God is perfectly known, loved, and glorified.

If St. Teresa and other saints have declared their readiness to suffer all tortures imaginable for the promotion of God's glory in a single degree, what should not we do and suffer for the deliverance of these souls from the flames of Purgatory, since by doing so we increase His glory by millions of degrees, and not for one moment only, but for eternity!

Prayer: Increase, O Lord! Thy honor and glory, that all created beings may praise Thy mercy forever, because Thou hast shown clemency towards the souls who love Thee and ardently desire to behold Thee. Comfort them, then, O Lord! Let them behold Thy face in the land of the blessed, where they shall honor, praise, and glorify Thee, world without end. Amen.

Special Intercession: Pray for the souls, who, while on earth, promoted the glory of God.

Eternal rest grant unto them, O Lord, and let perpetual light shine upon them; may they rest in peace. Amen. (Three times)

Practice: Make a good intention

before every work which you perform.

Invocation: My Jesus, mercy!

TWENTY-SEVENTH DAY.
THE LORD REWARDS CHARITY TOWARDS THE HOLY SOULS.

"Blessed are the merciful, for they shall obtain mercy." (Matth. v. 7.)

Theologians assert that those who bestow mercy upon the suffering souls, shall themselves find great relief and assistance in Purgatory; they consider active charity towards the holy souls a mark of predestination to eternal happiness. It is true, says St. Thomas Aquinas, that he who satisfies for the suffering souls does not satisfy for himself, but, it is also true, adds the saint, that he deserves more than the remission of pain, namely, eternal life. Hence it is that God Himself, by the mouth of the Royal Prophet, expresses Himself: "Blessed is he that understandeth concerning the needy and the poor: the Lord will deliver him in the evil day." (Ps. xl. 1.) The assistance of the holy souls is also experienced in temporal wants, in favor of their benefactors. Bishop Colmar of Mayence writes: "These destitute, suffering souls do not wait until they enter Heaven to exhibit their gratitude towards their benefactors: whilst they still languish in Purgatory, they pray without intermission for the welfare of soul and body, obtain for them recovery from disease, assistance in poverty, help in necessities, counsel and protection on journeys and in danger, preservation and increase of their temporal goods, aid them in the salvation of their souls, and, above all, come to their relief in the agonies of death and before the judgment-seat of God."

Prayer: We beseech Thee, O Lord! graciously hear the humble and fervent prayers we offer for the souls in Purgatory, and grant that the charity we extend towards our suffering brothers and sisters, may, by their supplications, obtain for us protection and help. Through Christ, our Lord. Amen.

Special Intercession: Pray for the souls who are suffering in Purgatory for their want of gratitude.

Eternal rest grant unto them, O Lord, and let perpetual light shine upon them; may they rest in peace. Amen. (Three times)

Practice: In spiritual and temporal wants, take refuge to the holy souls.

Invocation: My Jesus, mercy!

TWENTY-EIGHTH DAY.
THEY HAVE GREAT REASON TO FEAR, WHO SHOW NO MERCY TOWARDS THE SOULS DEPARTED.

"With what measure you mete, it shall be measured to you again." (Matth. vii. 2.) It will be readily seen that this word of the Divine Saviour is applicable also to the assistance we should render the souls departed. The learned Cardinal Cajetan says: "Those who in this life forget the departed, will, hereafter, in my opinion, be deprived in Purgatory of all participation in good works and devout prayers, though ever so many be offered for them by others; for Divine Justice is wont in this manner to punish their cruelty and hardness of heart." Hence, he who shows no mercy towards the suffering souls, and remains cold and indifferent to their pains, shall, even though his soul may have escaped eternal damnation, languish in the flames of Purgatory, without relief and consolation, and look in vain for friends and intercessors. The faithful, however, who do not forget the suffering souls completely, but seldom think of them, will not be deprived of friends and intercessors entirely, but will derive very little help and comfort, and their complaints will be answered by the words of St. Paul: "He who soweth sparingly, shall also reap sparingly." (2 Cor. ix. 6.)

Prayer: O God! Whose goodness and mercy are infinite, have pity on the souls of those, who, on account of their want of charity, are undeserving of Thy bounty, and accept our fervent prayers, in reparation for their faults, that they may not suffer without consolation. Through Christ, our Lord. Amen.

Special Intercession: Pray for the souls who suffer for their want of charity.

Eternal rest grant unto them, O Lord, and let perpetual light shine upon them; may they rest in peace. Amen. (Three times)

Practice: Bear patiently the ingratitude of others, and offer it for the souls in Purgatory.

Invocation: My Jesus, mercy!

TWENTY-NINTH DAY.

PERSEVERANCE IN PRAYERS FOR THE DEPARTED.

Holy Church, our good and tender mother, most ardently desires that her children be admitted to the beatific vision of God, and incessantly offers pious supplications, during the Holy Sacrifice of Mass and the Divine office, to obtain mercy for the holy suffering souls, thereby teaching us to think of them frequently; for to the end of time there shall be souls in the flames of Purgatory in need of assistance and fervent prayers, which we should never fail to offer in their behalf. The ways of God are often inscrutable, and His designs concerning the holy souls are unknown to us; hence there may be among their number some who have a just claim on our assistance, although a long time may have passed away since the close of their earthly career. Should the souls of our own beloved dead no longer be in need of our suffrages, they will be bestowed upon others, who are deserving of our mercy as well; thus, our prayer, our labor of love, will not be less salutary and meritorious, and, indeed, life is not too long for us to practise this genuine charity to the end.

Prayer: We beseech Thee, O Lord! grant us the grace to persevere in our charity towards the souls in Purgatory; deign to look with eyes of mercy upon these penitent souls; deliver them from their suffering, and open to them the portals of Heaven. Through Christ, our Lord. Amen.

Special Intercession: Pray for the souls who suffer for inconstancy in the service of God.

Eternal rest grant unto them, O Lord, and let perpetual light shine upon them; may they rest in peace. Amen. (Three times)

Practice: Examine how you have kept your good resolutions, particularly in what manner you have performed your devotions and works of charity for the suffering souls.

Invocation: My Jesus, mercy!

THIRTIETH DAY.
THE HEROIC ACT OF CHARITY FOR THE SOULS IN PURGATORY.

This heroic act, in behalf of the souls in Purgatory, consists in a voluntary offering made in their favor to the Divine Majesty, by any one of the faithful, of all works of satisfaction done by him in his life, as well as of all the suffrages which shall be offered for him after his death. By this offering he foregoes in their behalf only that special fruit which belongs to himself, so that he is not hindered thereby in praying for his own necessities, or those of others.

This act of charity, therefore, will not deprive us of any merit. Besides, by resigning our own claims on all works of satisfaction in favor of the souls departed, we shall gain for ourselves the special love of God, the Blessed Virgin Mary, and all the saints, according to the promise of Christ: "With what measure you mete, it shall be measured to you again." (Matth. vii. 2.) Furthermore, the gratitude of the holy souls will induce them, in turn, to pray for us in Heaven, so that we may either escape Purgatory, or be blessed by a speedy deliverance therefrom.

This heroic act of charity has been enriched with many indulgences. (No. 547.) They are as follows:

I. The Indult of a Privileged Altar, personally, every day in the year to all priests who shall have made this offering.

II. A Plenary Indulgence daily, applicable only to the departed, to all the faithful, who shall have made this offering, whenever they go to Holy Communion, provided they visit a church or public oratory, and pray there for some time for the intention of his Holiness.

III. A Plenary Indulgence, every Monday, to all who hear Mass in aid of the souls in Purgatory, provided they fulfill the other conditions mentioned above. (No. 547.)

Prayer: We humbly beseech Thee, O Lord! graciously accept our prayers, with the indulgences attached, for the suffering souls. We offer Thee, in their behalf, the Precious Blood of Jesus Christ, Thy Son, our Redeemer, and

His infinite merits united with the merits of His most holy, immaculate Virgin Mother Mary, her ever-glorious spouse, St. Joseph, the holy Apostles, and all the spirits of Heaven, that by virtue of these merits our devotion may be to them a source of consolation, and open to them the portals of Heaven, there to love, praise, and glorify Thee, world without end. Amen.

Special Intercession: Pray for the souls, who, while on earth, made the Heroic Act of Charity.

Eternal rest grant unto them, O Lord, and let perpetual light shine upon them; may they rest in peace. Amen. (Three times)

Practice: Endeavor, every day, to perform an act of charity for the suffering souls.

Invocation: My Jesus, mercy!

THIRTY-FIRST DAY.

BY A GOOD INTENTION TO MAKE EVEN OUR MOST TRIVIAL ACTIONS AND SUFFERINGS MERITORIOUS, AND OFFER THEM FOR THE DELIVERANCE OF THE HOLY SOULS.

As rational beings we should have a distinct object in view in all our actions. By performing even the most trivial act from the motive, thereby to please our dear Lord, and to do His holy will, they may become meritorious. It is understood that these acts are not contrary to the commandments of God and His holy Church, and that the person be in a state of grace. People who are working from early in the morning till late at night can assist the suffering souls in an efficacious manner by offering their toil and fatigue in union with the merits of Jesus and Mary for the relief of the suffering souls. Sick persons, and those enduring mental sufferings, such as temptations, scruples, contempt, slander, unjust treatment; those who mourn for the loss of a near relative or a dear friend, etc., may make the same intention in regard to their particular suffering.

Prayer: My dear Redeemer, how many occasions have I lost to gain merits by a good intention, and thus to assist Thy holy spouses! Pardon my negligence, and graciously assist me to turn every precious moment of time to advantage by a good intention, and to make up for the past. In union with Thy merits, and those of Thy holy Mother Mary and all the saints, I unite all my thoughts, words, deeds, and spiritual and bodily sufferings for the future, till my last breath, and offer them for the suffering souls. In return I beseech the holy souls to obtain for me, and all those for whom I am in duty and love bound to pray, spiritual and temporal favors, and abundant grace to lead a holy life and persevere to the end of their life. Through Christ, our Lord. Amen.

Special Petition: Pray for the souls who spent time uselessly, and were negligent in making and renewing the good intention.

Eternal rest grant unto them, O Lord, and let perpetual light shine upon them; may they rest in peace. Amen. (Three times)

Practice: When rising in the morning I shall never omit to make my good intention for the coming day, and to renew the same at least every hour, by saying: For love of Jesus and Mary, and the relief of the suffering souls.

Invocation: My Jesus, mercy!

A Short Meditation for Every Day.
The past—where is it?—It has fled.
The future?—It may never come.
Our friends departed?—With the dead.

Ourselves?—Fast hastening to the tomb.

What are earth's joys?—The dews of morn.

Its pleasures?—Ocean's writhing foam.

Where's peace?—In trials meekly borne.

Where's joy?—In Heaven, the Christian's home.

Morning Prayers.

By St. Alphonsus.

As soon as you awake, make the sign of the cross.

O my God, prostrate in Thy presence, I adore Thy boundless Majesty, I love Thine infinite goodness above all things, and I thank Thee with my whole heart for all the blessings Thou hast bestowed on me, and especially for having preserved me during the past night. I consecrate to Thee, in union with the merits of Jesus Christ, all my thoughts, all my words and works, and all the sufferings of this day; and I intend that every thought, word, and work, and suffering, shall be for Thy greater glory, and in honor of N——. (Make mention of a particular mystery or saint.)

I intend also to gain all the Indulgences that I can in favor of the souls in Purgatory.

O my God, for the love of Jesus Christ, preserve me from all sin. My Jesus, by Thy merits, grant that I may live always united to Thee. Mary, my Mother, bless me, and protect me under thy mantle. My Holy Guardian Angel, and all my Holy Patrons, intercede for me. Amen.

The Angelus.

(Recite the "Angelus" kneeling, except Saturday evening, and all Sunday.)

V. The angel of the Lord declared unto Mary.

R. And she conceived of the Holy Ghost.

Hail Mary.

V. Behold the handmaid of the Lord.

R. Be it done unto me according to Thy word.

Hail Mary.

V. And the Word was made flesh.

R. And dwelt among us.

Hail Mary.

V. Pray for us, O holy Mother of God.

R. That we may be made worthy of the promises of Christ.

Let us pray.

Pour forth, we beseech Thee, O Lord, Thy grace into our hearts, that we, to whom the incarnation of Christ Thy Son was made known by the message of an angel, may by His passion and cross be brought to the glory of His resurrection. Through the same Christ, our Lord. Amen.

May the divine assistance remain always with us.

And may the souls of the faithful departed through the mercy of God rest in peace. Amen.

INDULGENCE: Ten Years each time the Angelus or the Regina Coeli or Five Hail Marys are said in the morning, at noon and in the evening.

*PLENARY INDULGENCE under the usual conditions to those who recite this prayer every day for a month. (No. 300)

TO-DAY.

Dignare, Domine, die isto, sine peccato
    nos custodire.

Lord, for to-morrow and its needs
    I do not pray;
Keep me, my God, from stain of sin,
    Just for to-day.

Let me both diligently work
    And duly pray;
Let me be kind in word and deed,
    Just for to-day.

Let me be slow to do my will,
    Prompt to obey;
Help me to mortify my flesh,
    Just for to-day.

Let me no wrong or idle word
    Unthinking say;
Set Thou a seal upon my lips,
    Just for to-day.

Let me in season, Lord, be grave,
    In season gay;
Let me be faithful to Thy grace,
    Just for to-day.

And if to-day, my tide of life
    Should ebb away,
Give me Thy Sacraments Divine,
    Sweet Lord, to-day.

In Purgatory's cleansing fires
    Brief be my stay;
Oh, bid me, if to-day I die,
    Come home to-day.

So for to-morrow and its needs,
    I do not pray;
But guide me, guard me, keep me,
    Lord, just for to-day.

GOOD INTENTION.

SOLELY GOD'S GLORY.

All my work, throughout the day,
Every footstep on my way,
Every solace I may give,
Every want I may relieve,—
For Thy love, my God, shall be
Praise and honor, Lord, to Thee!
    Soli Deo Gloria.

All my labor, all my care,
Every burden I may bear,
Every word my lips disclose,
All my hours of sweet repose,
For Thy love, my God, shall be
Praise and honor, Lord, to Thee!
    Soli Deo Gloria.

Every word that I may write,
Every gleam of life and light,
Dawn of day,—its noon and night,
As life's moments onward glide,—
For Thy love, my God, shall be—
Praise and honor, Lord, to Thee!
    Soli Deo Gloria.

All my heart,—its hopes and fears,
Pain and sorrow, smiles and tears,
Every hour of joy and glee,
Every trial sent to me,—
For Thy love, my God, shall be—
Praise and honor, Lord, to Thee!
    Soli Deo Gloria.

When I take my meals each day,
Greet my friends upon my way,
Simply pluck a flowret sweet,
Stoop to take up dust, or weed,
For Thy love, my God, shall be—
Praise and honor, Lord, to Thee!
    Soli Deo Gloria.

Every labor, mean and lowly,
Every action great and holy,
Should the world its praise bestow
Or my angel, silent, know,—
For Thy love, my God, shall be—
Praise and honor, Lord, to Thee!
    Soli Deo Gloria.

When life's lamp has ceased to burn,
And my breaking eyes I turn
To Thy Cross, to bid farewell;
When my heart shall sound its knell,
Let my spirit, pure and free,
Sing Thy praise eternally!
    Soli Deo Gloria.

Renew your intention often during the day by saying: "All for love of Jesus and Mary, and for the relief of the suffering souls!"

Before Meals.

"Bless us, O Lord, and these Thy gifts which we are about to receive from Thy bounty. Through Christ, our Lord. Amen."

After Meals.

"We give Thee thanks, Almighty God, for all Thy benefits. Who livest and reignest, world without end. Amen."

"May the souls of the faithful departed through the mercy of God rest in peace! Amen.

Evening Devotions.

O Lord, my God, Who art present everywhere, I prostrate myself before Thee to adore Thee and praise Thee before I take my rest.

Deign to receive my heartfelt thanks for the blessings and graces Thou hast been pleased to give me this day. Enlighten my mind that I may know my own ingratitude, and move my will to bewail my sins and to amend them. Amen.

Examine your conscience about the sins, faults, and omissions of the past day.

An Act of Faith.

O my God! I firmly believe that Thou art one God in three Divine Persons, Father, Son, and Holy Ghost; I believe that Thy Divine Son became man, and died for our sins, and that He will come to judge the living and the dead. I believe these and all the truths which the Holy Catholic Church teaches, because Thou hast revealed them, Who canst neither deceive nor be deceived.

An Act of Hope.

O my God! relying on Thy infinite goodness and promises, I hope to obtain pardon for my sins, the help of Thy grace, and life everlasting, through the merits of Jesus Christ, my Lord and Redeemer.

An Act of Love.

O my God! I love Thee above all things, with my whole heart and soul, because Thou art all-good and worthy of all love. I love my neighbor as myself for the love of Thee. I forgive all who have injured me, and ask pardon of all whom I have injured.

An Act of Contrition.

O my God! I am heartily sorry for having offended Thee, and I detest all my sins, because I dread the loss of heaven and the pains of hell, but most of all because they offend Thee, my God. Who art all-good and deserving of all my love. I firmly resolve, with the help of Thy grace, to confess my sins, to do penance, and to amend my life.

MEMORARE.

Remember, O most gracious Virgin Mary, that never was it known that anyone who fled to thy protection, implored thy help, or sought thy intercession, was left unaided. Inspired with this confidence, I fly unto thee, O Virgin of virgins, my Mother. To thee I come; before thee I stand, sinful and sorrowful. O Mother of the Word Incarnate, despise not my petitions, but in thy clemency hear and answer me. Amen.

*Three years indulgence each time. (No. 309)

Mary, Mother of God and Mother of mercy, pray for us and for the departed.

*300 days indulgence. (No. 270)

O glorious St. Joseph, father and protector of virgins, faithful guardian to whom God entrusted Jesus, innocence itself, and Mary the Virgin of virgins, I beseech thee, I implore thee by Jesus and Mary, by that double charge so precious to thee, grant that I may be preserved from every stain, and that chaste in body and pure of heart I may ever serve Jesus and Mary in perfect purity. Amen.

*Three years each time. (No. 435)

Angel of God, my guardian dear, to whom His love commits me here, ever this day be at my side, to light and guard, to rule and guide. Amen.

*Three hundred days. Plenary once a month, and on the feast of the Guardian Angels. (No. 415)

Visit, we beseech Thee, O Lord, this Thy house and family, and drive far from it all the snares of the enemy. Let Thy Holy Angels dwell herein to keep us in peace, and may Thy blessing be always upon us. Through Christ, our Lord. Amen.

I take this repose in order to please Thee, and I intend to love and praise Thee each moment that I breathe, as the saints and elect praise and love Thee in Heaven.

Mary, my Mother, bless me, and protect me under thy mantle. My Angel Guardian, and all my holy Patrons, intercede for me.

3 Hail Marys in honor of the Immaculate Virgin Mary, and one Pater and Ave in honor of your patron saint.

Devotions for Confession.

Prayer to the Holy Ghost.

Come, O Holy Ghost, fill the hearts of Thy faithful, and kindle in them the fire of Thy love.

V. Send forth Thy Spirit, and they shall be created.

R. And Thou shalt renew the face of the earth.

Let us pray.

O God, Who hast taught the hearts of Thy faithful by the light of the Holy Spirit; grant us by the same Spirit, to relish what is right and evermore to rejoice in His consolation. Through Christ, our Lord. Amen.

Now make your examination of conscience.

Act of Contrition
after the Examination of Conscience.

O my God, I am most heartily sorry for all my sins, and I detest them above all things from the bottom of my heart, because they displease Thee, O my God, Who art most deserving of all my love, for Thy most amiable and adorable perfections. I firmly resolve, with the assistance of Thy grace, never more to offend Thee, and to amend my life. Increase my sorrow, O my God, and strengthen me in my resolution.

Ah, my Jesus, I see how much Thou hast done and suffered for me, and I have been so ungrateful to Thee. How many times, for the sake of some miserable pleasure or fancy, have I bartered away Thy grace, and have lost Thee, O God of my soul!

My dear God, pardon me: I am sorry; I grieve with my whole heart, and I hope for pardon from Thee, because Thou art infinite goodness. If Thou wert not infinite goodness, I should lose hope, and I should not even have the courage to ask Thee to have mercy on me.

Say seven Hail Marys in honor of Our Lady of Sorrows. After each Hail Mary recite the stanza.

> Bid me bear, O Mother blessed!
> On my heart the wounds impressed:
> Suffered by the Crucified.

*500 Days Indulgence each time. (No. 341)

Make frequent acts of contrition while waiting to go to Confession. Picture vividly to yourself, that the Priest represents our Lord Himself and accuse yourself of your sins and their necessary circumstances to the Priest as you would to our Lord Himself and follow the directions and advice the Confessor gives you.

After Confession.

"O God and Father of Heaven, prostrate on my knees before Thee,

I render Thee thanks for the great grace Thou hast granted me without any merit of mine. I now again possess Thy grace and favor. Through the holy sacrament of Penance, in the name of Jesus, all my sins have been forgiven. I am again become a child of God, through Jesus Christ, converted from the state of sin to the state of grace. Praise and thanks be to Thee, O God, for the sweet consolation that I now experience within myself! Strengthen me, that I may sin no more, and never again lose this consolation and peace of conscience, and may shun the occasion of sin.

Most Holy Virgin Mary, assist me. Thou art the Mother of perseverance; all my hope is in thee. "My Queen! My Mother! I give myself entirely to thee; and to show my devotion to thee, I consecrate to thee this day, my eyes, my ears, my mouth, my heart, my whole being, without reserve. Wherefore, good Mother, as I am thine own, keep me, guard me as thy property and possession."

Hail Mary, etc.

NO MORE SIN.

To sin bid adieu; for sinning is slaying
  Your Jesus anew.
Bid cursing adieu; for cursing is stabbing
  Your Jesus anew.
False swearing adieu; such oaths stain the honor
  Of Jesus anew.
To drink bid adieu; for drunkenness
  drowneth His friendship in you.
Obscenity adieu; for this brings on Jesus
  The scourges anew.
Bid slander adieu; this murders your neighbor
  And Jesus anew.
Bid rancor adieu; for hating one only
  Your love is not true.
Bid vengeance adieu; forgive or no pardon
  Has Jesus for you.
Bid scandal adieu; it snatches from Jesus
  The souls to Him due.
Yes, sin—sin, adieu—to Jesus we'll ever
  Be faithful and true.

Acts before Communion.

O my God, I offer this Holy Communion to atone for my sins, to obtain all graces necessary for salvation and perseverance to the end; also for the relief of the souls in Purgatory.

Act of Faith.

My Divine Lord, I firmly believe that I am going to receive in Holy Communion Thy Body ,Blood, Soul, and Divinity; I believe this, because Thou hast said it, and Thy Holy Church teaches it and therefore, I am ready to maintain this truth at the peril of my life.

Act of Humility.

O Divine Lord, how shall I dare approach Thee, who have so often offended Thee? Lord, Who art Thou, and who am I? Indeed, I know well who Thou art, that Thou givest Thyself to me; but O Lord, I am not worthy that Thou shouldst enter under my roof, yet speak only the word and my soul shall be healed.

Act of Contrition.

O my God, I am heartily sorry for having offended Thee, because Thou art infinitely good, infinitely worthy of being loved, and because sin displeases Thee; I firmly purpose, with the help of Thy holy grace, never more to offend Thee, to avoid the occasions of sin, and to live better for the time to come.

Act of Love.

O my Divine Jesus, Who hast loved me to such an excess as to die for me, and to give my Thy adorable Flesh as the food of my soul: I love Thee with my whole heart, and desire to live and die in Thy holy love.

Act of Desire.

Come, O my Beloved, come and take possession of my heart; I long for Thee; I sigh for Thee. Come, Lord Jesus, come!

Most holy Virgin, and my Mother Mary, behold I already approach to receive thy Son. Would that I had the heart and love with which thou didst communicate! Give me, this morning, thy Jesus, as thou didst give Him to the shepherds and the kings. I intend to receive Him from thy pure hands. Tell Him that I am thy servant and thy client, for He will thus look upon me with a more loving eye, and now that He is coming, will press me more closely to Himself.

PRAYER OF THE CHURCH.

"Lord Jesus Christ, Who didst say to

ACTS BEFORE COMMUNION

Thy Apostles, I leave you My peace, I give you My peace: regard not my sins, but the faith of Thy Church; and grant her that peace and unity which is agreeable to Thy will. Who livest and reignest forever and ever. Amen.

"Lord Jesus Christ, Son of the living God, Who according to the will of Thy Father, hast by Thy death, through the cooperation of the Holy Ghost given life to the world, deliver me by this Thy most sacred Body and Blood, from all my iniquities, and from all evils: and make me always adhere to Thy commandments, and never suffer me to be separated from Thee. Who livest and reignest with God the Father and the Holy Ghost, world without end. Amen.

"Grant that the participation of Thy Body, O Lord Jesus Christ, which I, though unworthy, presume to receive may not turn to judgment and condemnation; but, through Thy mercy, be a safeguard and remedy, both to soul and body; Who with God the Father in the unity of the Holy Ghost, livest and reignest God forever and ever. Amen. (No. 128.)

"I will take the bread of Heaven and call upon the name of our Lord."

Striking your breast with humility and devotion, say three times:

"Lord, I am not worthy that Thou shouldst enter under my roof; say but the word and my soul shall be healed."

While receiving Holy Communion, say within your heart:

May the Body and Blood of our Lord Jesus Christ preserve my soul to everlasting life. Amen.

(Immediately after Holy Communion do not read prayers from your book, but make interior acts of faith, hope, charity, adoration, and humility. Beg your divine and most bountiful guest for particular graces with great fervor, but do not forget the suffering souls in Purgatory.)

Acts after Communion.

"What return shall I make the Lord for all He has given me?

"Praising, I will call upon the Lord, and shall be saved from my enemies.

"Grant, O Lord, that what we have taken with our mouth, we may receive with a pure mind, that of a temporal gift it may become to us an eternal remedy.

"May Thy Body and Blood, O Lord, which I have received, cleave to my soul; and grant that no stain of sin may remain in me, who have been fed with this pure and holy Sacrament. Who livest and reignest world without end. Amen.

"O holy Banquet, in which Christ is received, His passion commemorated, the soul is filled with grace, and a pledge of future glory is given us."

"*V*. Bread from Heaven Thou hast given them.

"*R*. That contains all sweetness and delight.

"O God, Who in this wonderful Sacrament has left us a perpetual memorial of Thy passion; grant us, we beseech Thee, so to reverence the sacred mysteries of Thy Body and Blood, that we may continually perceive in our souls the fruit of Thy redemption. Who, with the Father and the Holy Ghost, livest and reignest ever one God, world without end. Amen."

Act of Petition.

O my soul, what art thou doing? The present is no time to be lost: it is a precious time, in which thou canst receive all the graces which thou askest. Seest thou not the eternal Father Who is lovingly beholding thee? For within thee He sees His beloved Son, the dearest object of

His love. Drive, then, far from thee all other thoughts; rekindle thy faith, enlarge thy heart, and ask for whatever thou willest.

Hearest thou not Jesus Himself, Who thus addresses thee: What wilt thou that I should do to thee?" (St. Mark x. 51.) O soul, tell me, what dost thou desire of me? I am come for the express purpose of enriching and gratifying thee; ask with confidence, and thou wilt receive all.

Ah! my most sweet Saviour, since Thou hast come into my heart in order to grant me graces, and desirest that I should ask Thee for them, I ask Thee not for the goods of the earth— riches, honors, or pleasures; but grant me, I beseech Thee, intense sorrow for the displeasure I have caused Thee. Impart to me so clear a light, that I may know the vanity of this world, and how deserving Thou art of love. Change this heart of mine, detach it from all earthly affections; give me a heart, conformable in all things to Thy holy will, that it may seek only for that which is more pleasing to Thee, and have no other desire than Thy holy love: "Create a clean heart in me, O God." (Ps. l. 12.)

I deserve not this grace; but Thou, my Jesus, deservest it, since Thou art come to dwell in my soul. I ask it of Thee through Thy merits, and those of Thy most holy Mother, and by the love which Thou bearest to Thy Eternal Father.

Here pause, to ask Jesus for some other particular grace for yourself, and for your neighbors. Do not forget poor sinners, nor the souls in Purgatory.

Eternal Father, Jesus Christ Himself, Thy Son, has said, "Amen, amen I say unto you, if you ask the Father anything in My name, He will give it you." For the love, then, of this Son, Whom I now hold within my breast, do Thou graciously hear me and grant my petition.

My most sweet Loves, Jesus and Mary, may I suffer for you, may I die for you; may I be all yours, and in nothing my own! May the Most Blessed Sacrament ever be thanked and praised!

"Blessed be the holy and Immaculate Conception of the Blessed Virgin Mary, Mother of God!"

*300 days' indulgence each time. (No. 324)

PRAYER OF ST. IGNATIUS.

Soul of Christ, sanctify me.
Body of Christ, save me.
Blood of Christ, inebriate me.
Water from the side of Christ, wash me.
Passion of Christ, strengthen me.
O good Jesus, hear me.
Within Thy wounds hide me.
Suffer me not to be separated from Thee.
From the evil one defend me.
At the hour of my death call me,

And bid me come to Thee,
That with Thy saints I may praise
    Thee.
For ever and ever. Amen.

*300 days indulgence. After Holy Communion 7 years. Plenary indulgence once a month. (No. 105)

PRAYER TO JESUS CRUCIFIED.
(To be recited before a Crucifix)

Look down upon me, good and gentle Jesus, before Thy face I humbly kneel, and with burning soul pray and beseech Thee to fix deep in my heart lively sentiments of faith, hope, and charity, true contrition for my sins, and a firm purpose of amendment; whilst I contemplate with great love and tender pity Thy five wounds and ponder over them within me, calling to mind the words which David, Thy prophet, said of Thee, my Jesus: *"They pierced my hands and*

my feet; they numbered all my bones."
—Ps. xxi. 17, 18.

Indulgence ten years. Plenary after Holy Communion under the usual conditions. (No. 171)

PRAYER FOR THE FAITHFUL DEPARTED.

O most compassionate Jesus! have mercy on the souls detained in Purgatory, for whose redemption Thou didst take upon Thee our nature and endure a bitter death. Mercifully hear their groanings; look with pity on the tears which they now shed before Thee, and by the virtue of Thy Passion release them from the pains due unto their sins. O most pitiful Jesus, let Thy precious Blood flow down into Purgatory, and refresh and revive the captive souls suffering there. Stretch out unto them Thy strong right hand, and bring them forth into the place of refreshment, light, and peace. Amen.

ALL FOR JESUS.

My Jesus, I need only Thee!
Thy holy will my joy shall be;
Thy pleasure, Lord, is *all* to me.
What is this world, compared to Thee?
Oh, guide me on my lonely way,
And grant my one desire, I pray:
That naught in life may ever rend
My heart from Thy sweet Sacrament!

My Jesus, I need only Thee!
Take what is near and dear to me;
My heart may pierce deep sorrow's spears,
'Twill love Thee more 'mid grief and tears.
While yielding all will free this heart
One only grace to me impart:
Oh, let me to my journey's end
Be near to Thy sweet Sacrament!

My Jesus, I need only Thee!
Should I be ill - so let it be;
Should I be poor - I'll love Thee more;
In misery - Thy will adore.
Take all - my comfort, peace and rest;
I humbly bow, Thou knowest best!
But, till in death my heart is rent,
Let me dwell near Thy Sacrament!

My Jesus, I need only Thee!
No place on earth brings joy to me;
This world no happiness can give,
In Thee alone my soul shall live.
Lord, when my last dread hour is nigh,
Then guide me to my home on high;
To me, when Angel Death is sent,
Oh, come, in Thy sweet Sacrament!

My Jesus, I need only Thee!
No sacrifice seems great to me;
Thy mandates e'er my joy shall be;
Lead Thou the way - I'll follow Thee.
Tho' I grow weak, still I rejoice;
Speak, Lord. Thy servant hears Thy voice!
But strengthen me, Thy child defend
In Thy sweet, Holy Sacrament!

My Jesus, Thou art all to me!
Here and beyond - eternally,—
For, what is Heaven's highest grace
But to behold Thee, face to face!
I cling to Thee! to Thee alone!
My God, my Love, my All, my Own!
Till I embrace Thee, without end,
My joy is here - Thy Sacrament.

Hearing Mass,

IN UNION WITH THE
PASSION OF JESUS CHRIST.

The Priest goes to the Altar.

Lord Jesus Christ, Son of the living God, Who, when Thy passion drew nigh, didst for me, a wretched sinner, fear and grow sad, grant that I may ever direct all my sorrows unto Thee, Who art the God of my heart; and Thou, O Lord, through Thy passion and sorrow, assist me to bear them with patience, that, by the merits of Thy sufferings, they may become profitable to my soul. Amen.

The Priest begins Mass.

Lord Jesus Christ, Son of the living God, Who in Thy bitter agony in the Garden wast comforted by an Angel, grant, through the merits of Thy prayer, that when I pray, Thy holy angel may assist and comfort me. Amen.

At the Confiteor.

Lord Jesus Christ, Who, praying in the garden unto Thy heavenly Father, in Thy agony, didst miraculously sweat blood from all Thy members, grant, that, by remembrance of Thy bitter passion, I may shed tears of sincere repentance now in Thy presence. Amen.

The Priest kisses the Altar.

Lord Jesus Christ, Who didst suffer Judas to betray Thee with a kiss, grant that I may never betray Thee in my neighbor or myself; nor ever return evil to my enemies, but the good offices of charity. Amen.

The Priest goes to the Epistle Side of the Altar.

Lord Jesus Christ, Who didst submit to be bound by the hands of wicked men, break, I beseech Thee, the chain of my sins, and so tie me with the bands of charity and the cords of Thy commandments, that I may neither in thought, word, nor deed, offend Thee hereafter. Amen.

At the Introit.

Lord Jesus Christ, Who wast brought as a criminal to Annas, by an armed band of wicked men, grant that I may never suffer myself to be led into sin by the evil suggestions of my fellow creatures, or the temptations of the wicked one, but that I may be safely guided by Thy Holy Spirit, to the fulfilment of Thy Divine will. Amen.

At the Kyrie Eleison.

Lord Jesus Christ, Who didst suffer Thyself to be thrice denied by the prince of the Apostles in the house of Caiphas, preserve me, I beseech Thee, from evil company, that I may suffer all worldly losses, and even death itself, rather than deny Thee once. Amen.

At the Dominus Vobiscum.

Lord Jesus Christ, Who, mercifully looking back on St. Peter, didst cause him to weep bitterly for his offences, look on me, I beseech Thee, with Thine eyes of mercy, that I may with tears fully bewail my sins, and neither in word nor deed ever offend Thee, my Lord and my God. Amen.

At the Epistle.

Lord Jesus Christ, Who didst submit to be brought before Pilate, and there falsely accused, teach me to avoid the snares of the wicked, and to profess my faith constantly by the performance of good works. Amen.

At the Munda Cor Meum.

Lord Jesus Christ, Who before Herod didst suffer for us sinners, grant that I may bear patiently the injuries inflicted on me, and learn from Thee, O my divine Master, to be meek and humble of heart. Amen.

At the Gospel.

Lord Jesus Christ, Who didst submit to be sent back as a fool by Herod to Pilate, and by that means, cause a reconciliation between them, strengthen me by Thy grace, that I may not fear the designs of my enemies, but profit by being persecuted by them, and imitate Thine example. Amen.

At the Unveiling of the Chalice.

Lord Jesus Christ, Who wast despoiled of Thy garments, and stripped naked, and scourged, for my sake, grant me grace, by a sincere confession of my sins, to put off the old man with all his acts, and never to appear before Thee destitute of the virtues of a Christian. Amen.

At the Offertory.

Lord Jesus Christ, Who for me wast pleased to be bound unto a pillar, and there cruelly scourged, give me grace willingly to bear the scourges of Thy paternal correction, and never more to grieve Thee by my sins. Amen.

At the Covering of the Chalice.

Lord Jesus Christ, Who didst for my sake submit to be cruelly crowned with thorns, pierce my heart so thoroughly with the thorns of penance, that I may deserve to be hereafter crowned by Thee in heaven. Amen.

The Priest Washes his Fingers.

Lord Jesus Christ, Son of the living God, Who though declared innocent by the Governor Pilate, didst hear, without opening Thy divine lips, the outcries of the Jews to crucify Thee, grant me grace to lead a holy life and not to be troubled by the opinions of men, to live innocently, and patiently to bear the malice of others. Amen.

At the Orate Fratres.

Lord Jesus Christ, Who without murmuring voluntarily didst submit to the cruel mocking of the Jews, grant me grace faithfully to resist all emotions of vain glory, and on the day of judgment to appear before Thee in the sacred garb of humility. Amen.

At the Preface.

Lord Jesus Christ, Who didst, for my sake, vouchsafe to receive the sentence of death, even the death of the cross, grant that on account of Thy love I may not fear the sentence of the most cruel death that the perverted judgments of men can pronounce against me, nor ever perversely judge others. Amen.

At the Memento for the Living.

Lord Jesus Christ, Who, for my salvation, didst carry on Thy shoulders Thy heavy cross, grant that I may ardently embrace the cross of mortification, and, for the love of Thee, bear it daily after Thee. Amen.

The Priest holds his Hands over the Chalice.

Lord Jesus Christ, Who, in that painful journey to Calvary, didst so lovingly admonish the holy women that wept over Thee, to mourn for themselves, give me grace to shed tears of repentance, that with them I may wash off my sins, and become acceptable to Thy Divine Majesty. Amen.

The Priest Signs the Oblation.

Lord Jesus Christ, Who wast for my sake nailed to the cross, and didst fasten thereto the handwriting of sin and death that was against me, pierce, I beseech Thee, my body with Thy holy fear, that, firmly adhering to Thy precepts, I may for ever be with Thee fastened to Thy cross. Amen.

The Elevation of the Host.

Lord Jesus Christ, Who, for love of me, wast pleased to be elevated on the cross and exalted above the earth, detach my heart, I beseech Thee, from all earthly affections, that my soul may always live in the contemplation of heavenly things. Amen.

At the Elevation of the Chalice.

Lord Jesus Christ, Thy saving wounds are the fountain of grace for us; grant that through the merits of Thy precious blood our hearts may be purified from all impure thoughts and affections, and that it may prove a remedy for my sins. Amen.

At the Memento for the Dead.

Lord Jesus Christ, Who, hanging on the cross, didst implore Thy heavenly Father for all mankind, even Thy crucifiers, give me, I beseech

Thee, the grace of humility and patience, that, according to Thy precepts and example, I may love my enemies, and do good to those who hate me. Amen.

At the Nobis Quoque Peccatoribus.

Lord Jesus Christ, Who didst so mercifully promise heaven to the penitent thief who humbly acknowledged his injustice, behold me, I beseech Thee, with the same eyes of mercy, that, now confessing my crimes, I may obtain pardon, and at the end of my life be strengthened with the hope to be with Thee in heaven. Amen

At the Little Elevation.

Lord Jesus Christ, Who didst endure such thirst for my sake, grant me grace to bear patiently for Thy sake all earthly privations, and to hunger and thirst for Thy heavenly kingdom, and here below for Thy

Word and Thy precious Body and Blood. Amen.

At the Pater Noster.

Lord Jesus Christ, Who from the cross didst recommend Thy Blessed Mother to the Beloved disciple, and the disciple to Thy Mother, I beseech Thee to receive me and protect me amidst all the troubles of this life. Amen.

At the Breaking of the Host.

Lord Jesus Christ, Who, for my sake, dying on the cross, didst commend Thy soul unto Thy Father, grant that, in this life, I may spiritually die with Thee, and in the hour of my death confide my soul unto Thee, Who livest and reignest God, world without end. Amen.

The Priest Puts Part of the Host into the Chalice.

Lord Jesus Christ, Who, after Thy

glorious victory over the power of the devil, didst descend into Limbo, to liberate the souls imprisoned there, apply, I beseech Thee, the virtue of Thy most precious Blood and passion to the faithful souls in Purgatory, that they may be received into the joys of Thy kingdom. Amen.

At the Agnus Dei.

Lord Jesus Christ, the meditation on Thy torments has excited many to repentance; I beseech Thee, through the efficacy of Thy most bitter passion and death, grant me perfect contrition for the offences of my past life, and grace to avoid sin in future. Amen.

At the Communion.

Lord Jesus Christ, Who wast pleased to be buried in a new monument, give me, O Lord my God, a new heart, that, dying in Thee, I may happily participate in the glory of Thy resurrection. Amen.

At the Ablution.

Lord Jesus Christ, Who for me, miserable sinner, wast by Joseph and Nicodemus embalmed with spices, and wrapped in white linen, grant me worthily to receive from Thy holy Altar Thy true and living Body in the holy Eucharist, and for ever entertain it in a true heart. Amen.

After Communion.

Lord Jesus Christ, Who didst rise triumphant out of a sealed monument, grant me grace to rise from the bondage of sin, to walk in newness of life, that when Thou, Who art my Judge, shalt appear, I may also be worthy to appear with Thee in glory. Amen.

At the Dominus Vobiscum.

Lord Jesus Christ, Who, after Thy resurrection, didst manifest Thyself to Thy beloved mother and disciples, to their great joy and consolation, mercifully grant me the grace, that, after this mortal life, I may with them rejoice in Thy heavenly kingdom, enjoying Thy presence for ever. Amen

At the Last Collect.

Lord Jesus Christ, Who didst vouchsafe, after Thy resurrection, to converse forty days with Thy disciples, and instruct them in all the mysteries of faith, teach me, I beseech Thee, the knowledge of those divine truths and strengthen my belief in them, according to Thy doctrine, and never to swerve in the least from Thy will. Amen.

At the Last Dominus Vobiscum.

Lord Jesus Christ, Who, after the term of forty days, didst ascend glorious and immortal into heaven, in the presence of Thy disciples, grant that my heart may, for Thy love, loathe all earthly things: attend only unto things eternal and pant, hunger and thirst after Thee, as the first and best of all blessings. Amen.

At the Gospel of St. John.

Lord Jesus Christ, Who didst send the Holy Ghost upon Thy disciples, while they were engaged in prayer, cleanse, I beseech Thee, my heart from all sin, that the same Holy Ghost may always dwell in it by His manifold gifts, and my soul be everlastingly comforted. Amen.

(Prayers after Mass see page 157)

Mass for the Dead.

The prayers given in this Method are compiled from the Missal, the Breviary, the Ritual and the works of St. Alphonsus Liguori.

At the Beginning of Mass.

Deliver me, O Lord, from eternal death on that tremendous day when the heavens and the earth shall be shaken, when Thou shalt come to judge the world with fire. Seized am I with trembling, and I fear for the approaching trial, and the wrath to come. Oh, that day, that day of wrath, of calamity, and misery; that great and bitter day, indeed, when Thou shalt come to judge the world with fire!

Eternal rest grant unto them, O Lord, and let perpetual light shine upon them, may they rest in peace. Amen.

The Confiteor.

I confess to Almighty God, to Blessed Mary ever Virgin, to Blessed Michael, the Archangel, to Blessed John the Baptist, to the holy Apostles Peter and Paul, to all the saints, and to you, Father, that I have sinned exceedingly in thought, word, and deed, through my fault, through my fault, through my most grievous fault; therefore I beseech the Blessed Mary ever Virgin, the Blessed Michael, the Archangel, the Blessed John the Baptist, the holy Apostles Peter and Paul, and all the saints, and you, Father, to pray to the Lord, our God, for me.

Then pray for pardon, thus:

May God have mercy on me, forgive my sins, and lead me to eternal life! May the almighty and merciful God grant me the pardon, absolution, and remission of all my sins!

Introit.

When the Priest mounts the steps of the altar, imagine you hear the souls in Purgatory repeating the following verses, as if to implore your prayers:

Have pity on me, have pity on me, at least, you my friends, because the hand of the Lord hath touched me. My flesh is consumed, my bones hath cleaved to my skin, and nothing but lips are left about my teeth. Have pity on me, have pity on me, at least you, my friends. (Job xix. 21.)

Then pray:

Eternal rest grant unto them, O Lord, and let perpetual light shine upon them; may they rest in peace. Amen.

Kyrie Eleison.

Lord, have mercy on them!
Christ, have mercy on them!
Lord, have mercy on them!

Repeat each three times.

The Collect.

O God, the Creator and Redeemer of all the faithful, give to the souls of Thy servants departed the remission of all their sins, that through the help of pious supplications, they may obtain the pardon which they have always desired. Who livest and reignest, world without end. Amen.

The Epistle.

In those days, the most valiant Judas, having made a gathering, sent twelve thousand drachms of silver to Jerusalem, for sacrifice to be offered for the sins of the dead, thinking well and religiously concerning the resurrection. (For if he had not hoped that they that were slain should rise again, it would have seemed superfluous and vain to pray for the dead.)

And because he considered that they who had fallen asleep with godliness had great grace laid up for them. It is, therefore, a holy and wholesome thought to pray for the dead, that they may be loosed from sins. (2 Mach. xii. 46.)

Gradual.

Grant to them eternal rest, O Lord, and let perpetual light shine upon them. The just shall be in everlasting remembrance; he shall not fear the evil hearing. (Ps. cxi.)

Tract.

Release, O Lord, the souls of all the faithful departed, from the bonds of their sins; and by the assistance of Thy grace, may they escape the sentence of condemnation, and enjoy the bliss of eternal light.

Here, sometimes, is said the following hymn. When you perceive it is not said at the altar, you may pass it over also, and go on to the Gospel.

DIES IRAE

Nigher still, and still more nigh,
Draws the day of prophecy.
Doom'd to melt the earth and sky.

Oh, what trembling there shall be
When the world its Judge shall see,
Coming in dread majesty!

Hark! the trumpet's thrilling tone
From sepulchral regions lone,
Summons all before the throne.

Time and death it doth appall,
To see the buried ages all
Rise to answer at the call.

Now the books are open spread;
Now the writing must be read.
Which condemns the quick and dead:

Now before the Judge severe,
Hidden things must all appear;
Naught can pass unpunished here.

What, shall guilty I then plead?
Who for me will intercede,
When the saints shall comfort need?

King of dreadful Majesty!
Who dost freely save and free;
Fount of Pity, save Thou me!

Recollect, O love divine!
'Twas for this lost sheep of Thine,
Thou Thy glory didst resign.

Satest wearied seeking me,
Sufferedst upon the Tree;
Let not vain Thy labor be.

Judge of justice, hear my prayer,
Spare me, Lord, in mercy spare,
Ere the reckoning-day appear.

Lo, Thy gracious face I seek;
Shame and grief are on my cheek·
Sighs and tears my sorrows speak.

Thou didst Mary's guilt forgive,
Didst the dying thief receive,
Hence doth hope within me live.

Worthless are my prayers, I know,
Yet, oh, cause me not to go
Into everlasting woe.

Severed from the guilty band,
Make me with Thy sheep to stand,
Placing me on Thy right hand.

When the cursed in anguish flee
Into flames of misery;
With the blest then call Thou me.

Suppliant in the dust I lie!
My heart a cinder, crushed and dry,
Help me, Lord, when death is nigh!

Full of tears, and full of dread,
Is the day that wakes the dead;
Calling all with solemn blast.

From the ashes of the past,
Lord of Mercy, Jesus blest,
Grant the faithful light and rest.
     Amen.

The Gospel.

At that time, Jesus said to the multitude of the Jews: Amen, amen, I say unto you that the hour cometh, and now is, when the dead shall hear the voice of the Son of God, and they that hear shall live. For as the Father hath life in Himself, so hath He given to the Son also to have life in Himself; and He hath given Him power to do judgment, because He is the Son of man. Wonder not at this, for the hour cometh wherein all that are in the graves shall hear the voice of the

Son of God; and they that have done good shall come forth unto the resurrection of life; but they that have done evil, unto the resurrection of judgment. (St. John v. 25-29.)

The Offertory.

O Lord Jesus Christ, King of Glory! deliver the souls of all the faithful departed from the flames of hell, and from the deep pit. Deliver them from the lion's mouth, lest hell swallow them, lest they fall into darkness; and let Thy standard-bearer, St. Michael, bring them into the holy light, which Thou hast promised of old to Abraham and his posterity. We offer Thee, O Lord, a sacrifice of praise and of prayer: accept it on behalf of the souls we commemorate this day, and let them pass from death to life.

Here make an offering also of your own death and sufferings in union with the Holy Sacrifice, thus:

O my God, I offer Thee also the

hour of my death, and all the pains I am destined to suffer from this moment until my last breath. Give me strength to bear them with perfect conformity to Thy will. I cheerfully offer Thee, moreover, all the pains which Thou shalt prepare for me in Purgatory.

It is just that the fire should punish in me all the insults I have offered to Thee. O holy prison, when shall I find myself shut up in thee, secure of never again being able to lose my God? O holy fire, when wilt thou purify me from so many stains, and render me worthy to enter the Land of bliss? I offer all these pains to Thy glory, uniting them with the bitter pains of Jesus' passion. Eternal Father! I sacrifice to Thee my life and my whole being. I entreat Thee to accept this my sacrifice, in union with and through the merits of this great sacrifice of Jesus Christ, Thy Son. Amen.

Almighty God, Who art the guardian of souls, the safeguard of salvation, and the confidence of all believers, look mercifully down upon us, and through the merits of Thy dear Son, Whose sacred Body we offer in this sacrifice, bless the graves of our departed friends, that those mortal bodies which there repose, after the course of this life is ended, may with their happy souls, at the great judgment day, be found worthy to participate in the rewards of eternal life.

Enter not, O Lord, into judgment with these Thy servants, for with Thee shall no man be justified except through Thee the remission of all his sins be granted unto him. We beseech Thee, therefore, let not the sentence of Thy justice lie heavy upon those whom the earnest prayer of Christian faith recmends to Thee; but rather, by the succor of Thy grace, may they be found worthy to escape the avenging judgment who were signed with the seal of the Holy Trinity while they lived.

Graciously regard, O Lord, these gifts which we offer Thee for the souls of the faithful departed, that by celestial remedies made pure, they may repose in Thy compassionate mercy. Through Jesus Christ Thy Son, our Lord. Amen.

When the Priest, turning towards the people, says: "Orate Fratres,—Pray, my Brethren," answer:

May the Lord receive this sacrifice from thy hands, to the praise and glory of His holy name, for the salvation of our souls, and for the repose of the faithful departed.

The Secret.

Look favorably down, O Lord, we beseech Thee, upon this sacrifice which we offer for the souls of Thy departed servants, that as Thou wast pleased to bestow on them the merit of Christian faith, Thou mayest also grant them its reward. Through Jesus Christ Thy Son, our Lord. Amen.

The Preface.

It is truly meet and right, just and salutary, that we should always and everywhere give thanks to Thee, O holy Lord, Almighty Father, everlasting God, through Christ our Lord: Who by dying hath destroyed death for us, and rising again hath renewed our life; and Who hath left us this tremendous sacrifice as a propitiation for our sins, and for the sins of the faithful departed. Mercifully grant, therefore, that they for whom it is offered this day may speedily be released from all their sufferings, and find eternal rest and perpetual light with Thee in paradise; that there we, with them, may praise and celebrate Thy Majesty, in company with all the Angels and Archangels, the celestial Powers, the blessed Seraphs, and the whole host of Heaven, who chant Thy glory, evermore repeating: Holy! Holy! Holy! is the Lord God of hosts! the heavens and the earth are full of Thy glory! Hosanna in the highest! Blessed is He Who cometh in the name of the Lord! Hosanna in the highest!

The Canon.

We therefore suppliantly beseech Thee, O Father of mercies, through Jesus Christ Thy Son, our Lord, graciously to accept and bless this holy Sacrifice, which we offer Thee; for the peace and prosperity of the Holy Catholic Church, for Thy servant, our Father, Pope N——, for our Bishop and Clergy, and for all Thy faithful Catholic people; for the living, that they may prepare for death, and for the dead that they may obtain eternal rest.

Memento of the Living.

Be mindful, O Lord, of Thy servants N—— and N——, (here pause and recommend to God any living friend for whom you feel urged to pray during this Mass), and of all those friends who are very near and very dear to me, and of all those who have asked for, or desire my prayers, or for whom I ought especially to pray; and so direct and strengthen them by Thy holy grace, during life, that at the hour of their death the enemy may not prevail against them. Through Jesus Christ our Lord.

O Almighty and merciful God! Who hast bestowed on the human race both the means of salvation and the gift of eternal life, look graciously upon us, Thy servants, and cherish these souls which Thou hast created, that in the hour of our departure, being free from stain of sin, we may merit to be borne aloft by the hands of the holy Angels to Thee, our Creator.

Accept, O Lord, we beseech Thee, this sacrifice which we offer Thee for the souls of the faithful departed, and grant to us also, who still remain, the grace of a happy death, that by it being purged of all our faults, we, who in this life are afflicted by the scourges of Thy dispensation, may receive our eternal rest in the life to come.

When the first sound of the bell announces that the Priest is about to begin the consecration, say:

O God, may this offering be blessed, and in every way acceptable and agreeable to Thee; and for our salvation's sake, and for the comfort of departed souls, be changed into the Body and Blood of Thy dear Son, our Lord Jesus Christ. Amen.

The Consecration.

At the elevation of the Sacred Host, reverently look up at it and say:

My Lord and my God!

Hail! true Body of Jesus Christ, my Saviour! Oh, bless and sanctify my soul!

Then add:

Give them eternal rest, O Lord.

At the elevation of the Chalice, say:

Hail! true Blood of Jesus, my Redeemer! Oh, wash me pure from all my sins!

Then add:

Give them eternal rest, O Lord. May they rest in peace.

After the Consecration.

Commemorating, therefore, O Lord, the blessed Passion of Jesus Christ, Thy Son, our Lord, His resurrection from the dead, and His glorious ascension into Heaven, we offer before the throne of Thy most excellent Majesty, in behalf of these departed souls, whom Thy justice still detains in the pains of temporal punishment, this most holy, pure, and unspotted victim, the holy bread of eternal life, and the chalice of everlasting salvation.

A Special Memento of the Dead.

Be mindful, especially, O Lord, of Thy servants, N—— and N——, who are gone before us with the sign of Faith, and rest in the sleep of peace. (Here make mention of those departed friends whom you wish in particular to recommend to the divine mercy.) To these and to all who sleep in Christ, grant, we beseech Thee, a place of refreshment, light, and peace. Through the same Christ, our Lord. Amen.

Grant, O Lord, to Thy servants departed that they may not receive a return of punishment for their deeds, who in desire were observers of Thy will; and that, as here true faith has joined them to the company of Thy faithful, so there Thy mercy may associate them to the choir of angels.

O God, Whose attribute it is always to show mercy and to spare, we humbly beseech Thee for the souls of

Thy faithful servants, whom Thou hast called out of this world, that Thou wouldst not deliver them into the hands of the enemy, nor forget them until the end, but command them to be received by the holy Angels, and so be led to Paradise, their true country; that as they have believed and hoped in Thee, they may not suffer the pains of hell, but possess everlasting joys.

O God, the light of faithful souls, be present to our supplications, and grant to all Thy servants and handmaids whose bodies rest in Christ, a seat of refreshment, a blissful rest, and the light of glory.

We humbly pour out our prayers to Thee, O Lord, for these Thy servants beseeching Thee, that whatever guilt they may have contracted through human frailty, Thou wilt mercifully pardon, and place them in the seat of those happy souls whom Thou hast redeemed. Through Jesus Christ, our Lord.

To us also, sinners though we are, yet Thy servants, and trusting in the multitude of Thy mercies, deign to grant some part and fellowship with all Thy saints. Into their company, we beseech Thee, graciously to admit us, not weighing our merits, but Thy mercy. Through Christ, our Lord. Amen.

Pater Noster.

Repeat with the Priest: "Our Father Who art in Heaven," etc.; and then offer the following petition:

Deliver, O Lord, I beseech Thee, the souls of Thy servants from all sorrow and suffering, and bring them to the participation of Thy heavenly joys, and through the intercession of the blessed and glorious Mary, ever Virgin, Mother of God, of the holy Apostles Peter and Paul and Andrew, and of all the saints, mercifully grant to me also the pardon of my sins, grace to the remnant of my days, and peace in the hour of my death, that so through the help of Thy mercy, in the awful hour of judgment I may stand before the face of my accusing enemy without alarm. Through Jesus Christ, Thy Son, our Lord. Amen.

Agnus Dei.

At the "Agnus Dei," pray thus:

Lamb of God, Who takest away the sins of the world! *Grant them rest.*

Lamb of God, Who takest away the sins of the world! *Grant them rest.*

Lamb of God, Who takest away the sins of the world! *Grant them eternal rest.*

O Lord Jesus Christ, Son of the living God, Who according to Thy Father's will, and by the cooperation of the Holy Ghost, hast given life to the world through Thine own death, deliver me by this, Thy most sacred Body and Blood, from all my sins, and from every evil; make me always cling to Thy commandments, and never let me be separated from Thee.

O Almighty and merciful God! I beseech Thee, may all these Sacraments in which it is our privilege to participate, be the means of our purification; and grant that this Thy Sacrifice may not be to us a ground of accusation for our punishment, but a salutary intercession for our pardon; may it serve for the washing away of our guilt, for the strengthening of our frailty, and for a support against all the dangers of the world, and to all Thy faithful people, whether living or dead, for the remission of all their sins. Through Jesus Christ, our Lord. Amen.

The Communion.

At the signal given with the little bell, when the Priest, before receiving the Sacred Host, strikes his breast three times, do the same, and say each time:

Lord! I am not worthy that Thou shouldst enter under my roof, but only speak the word, and my soul shall be healed. (No. 129.)

Here go to Holy Communion or at least make a spiritual Communion, uniting yourself in desire with the Communion of the Priest. After which, recite the following prayer:

To Almighty God, O dear departed Brethren, we now commend you. May the bright company of the Angels come to seek you; may the senate of the Apostles come to greet you; may the triumphant army of glorious Martyrs come to meet you; the glittering throng of Confessors encompass you with their lilies in their hands; the choir of Virgins receive you with songs of joy; and a happy rest embrace you on the bosoms of the Patriarchs.

THE LAST GOSPEL.

For the last Gospel, read what follows:

I know that my Redeemer liveth, and in the last day I shall rise out of the earth; and I shall be clothed again with my skin, and in my flesh I shall see my God: Whom I, myself, shall see, and my eyes shall behold, and not another. This my hope is laid up for me in my bosom. (Job xix. 25.) I am the Resurrection and the Life; he that believeth in Me, although he be dead, shall live; and every one that liveth and believeth in Me, shall not die forever. (St. John xi. 25.) And I heard a voice saying unto me: Write: Blessed are the dead who die in the Lord. From henceforth now, saith the Spirit, that they may rest from their labors: for their works follow them. (Apoc. xiv. 13.)

R. Thanks be to God.

Prayers after Mass.

Salve Regina.

Hail! Holy Queen, Mother of Mercy, our life, our sweetness, and our hope! To thee do we cry, poor banished children of Eve; to thee do we send up our sighs, mourning and weeping in this valley of tears! Turn, then, most gracious Advocate, thine eyes of mercy towards us, and after this, our exile, show unto us the blessed fruit of thy womb, Jesus. O clement, O loving, O sweet Virgin Mary!

V. Pray for us, O Holy Mother of God.

R. That we may be made worthy of the promises of Christ.

Let us pray.

O God, our refuge and our strength, look down with favor upon Thy people, who cry to Thee; and through the intercession of the glorious and immaculate Virgin Mary, Mother of God, of her Spouse, Blessed Joseph, of Thy holy Apostles, Peter and Paul, and all the saints, mercifully and graciously hear the prayers which we pour forth to Thee, for the conversion of sinners, and the liberty and exaltation of Holy Mother Church. Through the same Christ, our Lord. Amen.

St. Michael, the Archangel, defend us in battle; be our protection against the malice and snares of the devil. We humbly beseech God to command him: and do thou, O Prince of the heavenly hosts, by the divine power thrust into hell Satan and the other evil spirits who roam through the world seeking the ruin of souls. Amen.

The faithful who devoutly recite these prayers kneeling, with the priest who has just celebrated a private Mass at which they have assisted are granted an Indulgence of ten years.

Most Sacred Heart of Jesus, have mercy on us. (Three times.)

Indulgence 7 years when added to the prayers after Mass. (No. 628)

Acts to be made at a Visit to the Most Blessed Sacrament.

(By St. Alphonsus.)

"My Lord, Jesus Christ, Who for the love which Thou bearest to men, remainest day and night in this Sacrament, full of compassion and of love, awaiting, calling, and welcoming all who come to visit Thee; I believe that Thou art present in the Sacrament of the Altar. I adore Thee from the abyss of my nothingness, and I thank Thee for all the graces which Thou hast bestowed upon me, and in particular for having given me Thyself in this Sacrament, for having given me Thy most holy Mother Mary as my advocate, and for having called me to visit Thee in this church. I now salute Thy most loving Heart; and this for three ends: 1. In thanksgiving for this great gift; 2. To make amends to Thee for all the outrages which Thou receivest in this Sacrament from all Thine enemies; 3. I intend by this visit to adore Thee in all the places on earth in which Thou art present in this Sacrament, and in which Thou art the least revered and the most abandoned. My Jesus, I love Thee with my whole heart; I grieve for having hitherto so many times offended Thy infinite goodness. I purpose by Thy grace never more to offend Thee for the time to come; and now, miserable and unworthy though I be, I consecrate myself to Thee without reserve; I give Thee and renounce my entire will, my affections, my desires, and all that I possess. From henceforward do Thou dispose of me and all that I have as Thou pleasest. All that I ask of Thee and desire is Thy holy love, final perseverance, and the perfect accomplishment of Thy will. I recommend to Thee the souls in Purgatory, but especially those who had the greatest devotion to the Most Blessed Sacrament, and to the most Blessed Virgin Mary.

"I also recommend to Thee all poor sinners. In fine, my dear Saviour, I unite all my affections with the affections of Thy most loving Heart, and I offer them, thus united, to Thy Eternal Father, and beseech Him in Thy Name to vouchsafe, for Thy love, to accept and grant them."

*Indulgence of five years if recited before the Blessed Sacrament. (No. 153)

Spiritual Communion.

"My Jesus, I believe that Thou art present in the most Holy Sacrament. I love Thee above all things, and I desire to receive Thee into my soul. Since I can not now receive Thee sacramentally, come at least spiritually into my heart. I embrace Thee, as if Thou wert already there, and unite myself wholly to Thee; never permit me to be separated from Thee."

3 years. Any form. (No. 135.)

DIVINE PRAISES.

Blessed be God.

Blessed be His Holy name.

Blessed be Jesus Christ, true God and true man.

Blessed be the name of Jesus.

Blessed be His Most Sacred Heart.

Blessed be Jesus in the most holy Sacrament of the Altar.

Blessed be the great Mother of God, Mary most holy.

Blessed be her holy and Immaculate Conception.

Blessed be the name of Mary, Virgin and Mother.

Blessed be St. Joseph, her most chaste spouse.

Blessed be God in His Angels and in His Saints.

*Three years' indulgence. Indulgence of five years if recited publicly. (No. 646)

Daily Offering to the Sacred Heart of Jesus.

O Lord Jesus Christ, in union with that divine intention with which Thou, whilst on earth, didst give praise to God through Thy most Sacred Heart, and which Thou dost still everywhere offer to Him in the Holy Eucharist, even to the consummation of the world, I, in imitation of the most sacred heart of the ever immaculate Virgin Mary, do most cheerfully offer Thee, during this entire day, all my thoughts and intentions, all my affections and desires, my words, and all my works.

Prayer for the Faithful in their Agony.

Most merciful Jesus, lover of souls! I pray Thee by the agony of Thy most Sacred Heart, and by the sorrows of Thy immaculate Mother, wash in Thy Blood the sinners of the whole world who are now in their agony, and are to die this day. Amen.

Heart of Jesus, once in agony, pity the dying.

Three hundred days' indulgence. Plenary indulgence under usual conditions if recited three times a day for a month at different hours of the day. (No. 625)

Litany of the Sacred Heart of Jesus.

Lord, have mercy on us. *Christ, have mercy on us.*
Lord, have mercy on us.
Christ, hear us. *Christ, graciously hear us.*

God, the Father of Heaven,
God the Son, Redeemer of the world,
God the Holy Ghost,
Holy Trinity, one God,
Heart of Jesus, Son of the Eternal Father,
Heart of Jesus, formed by the Holy Ghost in the womb of the Virgin Mother,
Heart of Jesus, substantially united to the Word of God,
Heart of Jesus, of infinite Majesty
Heart of Jesus, Sacred Temple of God,
Heart of Jesus, tabernacle of the Most High,
Heart of Jesus, House of God and Gate of Heaven,
Heart of Jesus, burning furnace of charity,

Have mercy on us

LITANY OF THE SACRED HEART

Heart of Jesus, abode of justice and love,
Heart of Jesus, full of goodness and love,
Heart of Jesus, abyss of all virtues,
Heart of Jesus, most worthy of all praise,
Heart of Jesus, King and centre of all hearts,
Heart of Jesus, in Whom are all the treasures of wisdom and knowledge,
Heart of Jesus, in Whom dwells the fulness of divinity,
Heart of Jesus, in Whom the Father was well pleased,
Heart of Jesus, of Whose fulness we have all received,
Heart of Jesus, desire of the everlasting hills,
Heart of Jesus, patient and most merciful,
Heart of Jesus, enriching all who invoke Thee,
Heart of Jesus, fountain of life and holiness,
Heart of Jesus, **propitiation** for our sins,
Heart of Jesus, loaded down with opprobrium,
Heart of Jesus, bruised for our offences,

Have mercy on us

LITANY OF THE SACRED HEART

Heart of Jesus, obedient unto death,
Heart of Jesus, pierced with a lance,
Heart of Jesus, source of all consolation,
Heart of Jesus, our life and resurrection,
Heart of Jesus, our peace and reconciliation,
Heart of Jesus, victim for sin,
Heart of Jesus, salvation of those who hope in Thee,
Heart of Jesus, hope of those who die in Thee,
Heart of Jesus, delight of all the saints,

} *Have mercy on us*

Lamb of God, Who takest away the sins of the world, *spare us, O Lord.*
Lamb of God, Who takest away the sins of the world, *graciously hear us, O Lord.*
Lamb of God, Who takest away the sins of the world, *have mercy on us.*

V. Jesus meek and humble of heart,
R. Make our hearts like unto Thine.

Let us pray.

O Almighty and eternal God, look on the Heart of Thy most beloved Son, and on the praise and satisfaction It renders Thee in the name of sinners, and, being appeased, grant pardon to them imploring Thy mercy, in the name of the same Jesus Christ, Thy Son, who liveth and reigneth with Thee, world without end. Amen.

*Seven years' indulgence. (No. 213) Plenary indulgence once a month under the usual conditions. (No. 213)

Consecration of the Human Race to the Sacred Heart of Jesus.

Most Sweet Jesus, Redeemer of the human race, look down upon us, humbly prostrate before Thy altar. We are Thine, and Thine we wish to be; but to be more surely united with Thee, behold each one of us freely consecrates himself to-day to Thy most Sacred Heart. Many, indeed, have never known Thee; many, too, despising Thy precepts, have rejected Thee. Have mercy on them all, most merciful Jesus, and draw them to Thy Sacred Heart. Be Thou King, O Lord, not only of the faithful who have never forsaken Thee, but also of the prodigal children who have abandoned Thee; grant that they may quickly return to their Father's house, lest they die of wretchedness and hunger. Be Thou King of those who are deceived by erroneous opinions, or whom discord keeps aloof, and call them back to the harbor of truth and unity of faith, so that soon there may be but one flock and one Shepherd. Be Thou King of all those who are still involved in the darkness of idolatry or of Islamism, and refuse not to draw them all into the light and kingdom of God. Turn Thine eyes of mercy toward the children of that race, once Thy chosen people. Of old they called down upon themselves the Blood of the Saviour; may It now descend upon them a laver of redemption and of life. Grant, O Lord, to Thy Church assurance of freedom and immunity from harm; give peace and order to all nations, and make the earth resound from pole to pole with one cry: Praise to the Divine Heart that wrought our salvation; to It be glory and honor forever. Amen.

Five years. (No. 253.)
(Authorized by Pope Pius XI, Oct. 17, 1925)

Acts to be made at a Visit to the Blessed Virgin Mary.

(*By St. Alphonsus.*)

"Most Holy Immaculate Virgin, and my Mother Mary, to thee who art the Mother of my Lord, the Queen of the world, the Advocate, the Hope, and the Refuge of sinners, I have recourse to-day, I who am the most miserable of all. I render thee my most humble homages, O great Queen, and I thank thee for all the graces thou hast conferred on me until now; particularly for having delivered me from hell, which I have so often deserved. I love thee, O most amiable Lady and for the love which I bear thee, promise to serve thee always, and to do all in my power to make others love thee also. I place in thee all my hopes; I confide my salvation to thy care. Accept me for thy servant, and receive me under thy mantle, O Mother of mercy.

And since thou art so powerful with God, deliver me from all temptations, or rather obtain for me the strength to triumph over them until death. Of thee I ask a perfect love for Jesus Christ. Through thee I hope to die a good death. O my Mother, by the love which thou bearest to God, I beseech thee to help me at all times, but especially at the last moment of my life. Leave me not, I beseech thee, until thou seest me safe in Heaven, blessing thee and singing thy mercies for all eternity. Amen. So I hope. So may it be.

*Three years' indulgence if recited before an image of the Blessed Virgin. (No. 312)

The Magnificat; or, Canticle of the Blessed Virgin.

My soul doth magnify the Lord.
And my spirit hath rejoiced in God my Saviour.

Because He hath regarded the humility of His handmaid; for behold from henceforth all generations shall call me blessed.

Because He that is mighty hath done great things unto me; and holy is His name.

And His mercy is from generation to generation; unto them that fear Him.

He hath showed might in His arm; He hath scattered the proud in the conceit of their heart.

He hath put down the mighty from their seat; and hath exalted the humble.

He hath filled the hungry with good things; and the rich He hath sent empty away.

He hath received Israel His servant; being mindful of his mercy.

As He spoke to our fathers: to Abraham and to His seed forever.

Glory be to the Father, etc.

*Three years' indulgence. (No. 291)

Litany of the Blessed Virgin Mary

Lord, have mercy on us.

Christ, have mercy on us.

Lord, have mercy on us.

Christ, hear us.

Christ, graciously hear us.

God the Father of heaven, *have mercy on us.*

God the Son, Redeemer of the world, *have mercy on us.*

God the Holy Ghost, *have mercy on us*

Holy Trinity, one God, *have mercy on us.*
Holy Mary, *pray for us.*
Holy Mother of God, *pray for us.*
Holy Virgin of virgins,
Mother of Christ,
Mother of Divine grace,
Mother most pure,
Mother most chaste,
Mother inviolate,
Mother undefiled,
Mother most amiable,
Mother most admirable,
Mother of Good Counsel,
Mother of Perpetual Help,
Mother of our Creator,
Mother of our Saviour,
Virgin most prudent,
Virgin most venerable,
Virgin most renowned,
Virgin most powerful,
Virgin most merciful,
Virgin most faithful,
Mirror of justice,
Seat of wisdom,
Cause of our joy,
Spiritual vessel, } *Pray for us*

Vessel of honor,
Singular vessel of devotion,
Mystical rose,
Tower of David,
Tower of ivory,
House of gold,
Ark of the covenant,
Gate of heaven,
Morning star,
Health of the sick,
Refuge of sinners,
Comforter of the afflicted,
Help of Christians,
Queen of Angels,
Queen of Patriarchs,
Queen of Prophets,
Queen of Apostles,
Queen of Martyrs,
Queen of Confessors,
Queen of Virgins,
Queen of all Saints,
Queen conceived without original sin,
Queen of the most holy Rosary,
Queen of Peace,

} *Pray for us*

Lamb of God, Who takest away the sins of the world, *spare us, O Lord!*

Lamb of God, Who takest away the sins of the world, *graciously hear us, O Lord!*

Lamb of God, Who takest away the sins of the world, *have mercy on us, O Lord!*

Christ, hear us.

Christ, graciously hear us.

Anthem.

We fly to thy patronage, O holy Mother of God; despise not our prayers in our necessities but deliver us from all dangers, O glorious and ever blessed Virgin.

V. Pray for us, O holy Mother of God.

R. That we may be made worthy of the promises of Christ.

Let us Pray.

Grant, we beseech Thee, O Lord, unto all Thy servants that they may remain continually in the enjoyment of health, both of mind and body, and through the glorious intercession of the blessed Mary ever Virgin, may be delivered from present sadness, and enter into the joy of eternal happiness. Amen.

*Seven years' indulgence. (No. 290)

"Jesus, Mary and Joseph."

*Seven years' indulgence. (No. 256)

The Mysteries of the Holy Rosary.

The Joyful Mysteries.

To be said on Monday, Thursday, and during the time of Advent, Christmas and Octave of Epiphany, inclusively.

Whom thou, O Virgin, didst conceive.

Whom thou didst carry to Elizabeth.

Who was born of thee, O Virgin.

Whom thou didst present in the temple.

Whom thou didst find in the temple.

The Sorrowful Mysteries.

To be said on Tuesday, Friday, and during Lent.

Who sweat blood for us.
Who was scourged for us.
Who was crowned with thorns for us.
Who carried the heavy cross for us.
Who was crucified for us.

The Glorious Mysteries.

To be said Wednesday, Saturday and Sunday, and during paschal time.

Who arose from the dead.
Who ascended to Heaven.
Who sent the Holy Ghost.
Who assumed thee, O Virgin, into Heaven.
Who crowned thee, O Virgin, in Heaven.

To obtain the grace of perseverance, say the "Salve Regina," page 157.

V. Pray for us, O holy Mother of God.

R. That we may be made worthy of the promises of Christ.

Let us Pray.

(Prayer of the Church.)

O God, Whose only-begotten Son, by His life, death, and resurrection, has purchased for us the rewards of eternal life grant, we beseech Thee, that meditating upon these mysteries in the most holy Rosary of the Blessed Virgin Mary, we may imitate what they contain, and obtain what they promise. Through the same Christ, our Lord. Amen.

Rosary of the Blessed Virgin.

Blessed by the Canons Regular (Crosier-Fathers) of the Holy Cross in Europe.

An Indulgence of 500 days can be gained for every single "Our Father," or "Hail Mary," recited devoutly on one of these beads, without it being necessary to say the five decades or to meditate upon the mysteries. This Indulgence is applicable to the souls in Purgatory. The faculty to attach these special indulgences to Rosaries, was given by three Sovereign Pontiffs to the Canons Regular of St. Augustine of the Order of the Holy Cross and confirmed by Pope Leo XIII. March 14, 1884 who moreover declared this faculty to belong to the said Order.

Here it may be well to add a few words on Rosaries in general. When Rosaries are re-chained the indulgences remain, even if the beads are not placed in the same order as before. The indulgences also remain when unblessed beads are put in for broken or lost beads, provided at the time they are put in, the unblessed beads are less in number than the old beads left in the Rosary. But when the Rosaries are sold or utterly destroyed the indulgences are lost.

The indulgences of both the Crosier beads and of the Dominican Rosary can be gained by one recitation of the Rosary, provided the Rosary has both indulgences attached to it. (Pius X. June 12, 1907.)

A plenary indulgence may be gained by reciting five decades of the rosary in presence of the Blessed Sacrament. This indulgence can be gained each time the rosary is said in the presence of the Blessed Sacrament. The Blessed Sacrament does not have to be exposed to gain this indulgence. (No. 360)

Chaplet or Beads of the Seven Dolors.

(Before reciting the Seven Dolor Beads, it is recommended that you make an Act of Contrition.)

This is a devotion instituted in the course of the thirteenth century, in honor of the sorrows of the Blessed Virgin Mary, endured by her in compassion for the suffering and death of her Divine Son. It is practised upon a Chaplet composed of seven times seven beads, each portion of seven being divided from the rest by medals, representing the seven principal sorrows of her life. In the use of it a *Hail Mary* has to be said on each of the beads, with one *Our Father* before every seven *Hail Marys;* and at the end of all, three *Hail Marys* are to be said, in honor of the sorrowful tears of our Lady.

While reciting the first *Our Father,* and seven *Hail Marys,* reflect on and sympathize in the sorrow of our Blessed Lady, when she presented her Divine Child in the Temple, and heard from the aged Simeon that a sword of grief should pierce her soul on His account.

Our Father, seven *Hail Marys.*

At the second medal, reflect on her sorrow when, to escape the cruelty of King Herod, she was forced to fly into Egypt with St. Joseph and her Divine Child.

Our Father, seven *Hail Marys*.

At the third medal, reflect on her grief when, in returning from Jerusalem, she perceived that she had lost her dear Jesus, Whom she sought sorrowing during three days.

Our Father, seven *Hail Marys*.

At the fourth, reflect on her meeting her Divine Son, all bruised and mangled, carrying His cross to Calvary, and seeing Him fall under His heavy weight.

Our Father, seven *Hail Marys*.

At the fifth, reflect on her standing by when her Divine Son was lifted up no the cross, and the Blood flowed in streams from His sacred Wounds.

Our Father, seven *Hail Marys*.

At the sixth, reflect on her sorrow when her Divine Son was taken down from the cross, and she received Him into her arms.

Our Father, seven *Hail Marys*.

Seventhly, and lastly, contemplate her following His sacred Body, as it was borne by Joseph of Arimathea and Nicodemus, to the sepulchre, inclosed there, and hidden from her sight.

Our Father, seven *Hail Marys*.

Three *Hail Marys*, as mentioned above, in honor of her tears.

INDULGENCES.

All Indulgences previously granted for the recitation of the Seven Dolors Rosary were withdrawn by the Holy See in 1934 and the following Indulgences were granted:

1) an Indulgence of five years as often as this rosary is recited;

2) an Indulgence of ten years if it is recited on Friday or if it is recited with others, or if the recitation is joined to some good work, as hearing Mass or a sermon;

3) a Plenary Indulgence once a month, if the rosary is recited daily;

4) a Plenary Indulgence to those who recite this rosary on the two feasts of Our Lady of Sorrows. (Friday of Passion Week and Sept. 15.)

In private recitation the whole chaplet need not be recited at one time; each one of the so-called dolors may be said at different times during the day.

LAY BAPTISM.

Take common water, pour it on the face of the child, and while you are pouring it, say the following words:

"I baptize thee in the name of the Father, and of the Son, and of the Holy Ghost."

NOTE: Any person whether man, woman, or child, may baptize an infant in case of danger of death.

PRAYERS EVERY CATHOLIC SHOULD KNOW BY HEART

The Sign of the Cross.

In the name of the Father, and of the Son, and of the Holy Ghost. Amen.

The Doxology.

Glory be to the Father, and to the Son, and to the Holy Ghost. As it was in the beginning, is now, and ever shall be, world without end. Amen.

The Lord's Prayer.

Our Father, who art in heaven, hallowed be Thy name; Thy Kingdom come; Thy will be done on earth as it is in heaven. Give us this day our daily bread; and forgive us our trespasses as we forgive those who trespass against us: and lead us not into temptation but deliver us from evil Amen.

The Angelical Salutation.

Hail Mary, full of grace! the Lord is with thee: blessed art thou amongst women, and blessed is the fruit of thy womb, Jesus. Holy Mary, Mother of God, pray for us sinners, now and at the hour of our death. Amen.

The Apostles' Creed.

I believe in God, the Father Almighty, Creator of heaven and earth; and in Jesus Christ, His only Son, our Lord; who was conceived by the Holy Ghost, born of the Virgin Mary, suffered under Pontius Pilate, was crucified; died, and was buried. He descended into hell: the third day He arose again from the dead: He ascended into heaven, sitteth at the right hand of God, the Father, Almighty; from thence He shall come to judge the living and the dead. I believe in the Holy Ghost, the Holy Catholic Church, the communion of Saints, the forgiveness of sins, the resurrection of the body, and the life everlasting. Amen.

SIX TRUTHS WHICH WE MUST KNOW AND BELIEVE.

1. There is only *one* God who created all things, and Who preserves and governs all things.

2. God is a just Judge, Who rewards the good and punishes the wicked.

3. In God there are three Persons: the Father, the Son and the Holy Ghost.

4. The second Person of the Blessed Trinity became man, to redeem us by His death and to make us eternally happy.

5. The soul is immortal.

6. The grace of God is necessary for salvation.

PRAYER TO CHRIST THE KING.

O Christ Jesus, I acknowledge Thee as Universal King. For Thee all creatures have been made. Do Thou exercise over me all Thy rights. Renewing my baptismal vows, I renounce Satan, with all his works and pomps and I promise to live as a good Catholic. Especially do I pledge myself to work with all my power for the triumph of the rights of God and of Thy Church.

Divine Heart of Jesus, I offer Thee all my poor actions to obtain that all hearts may recognize Thy Sacred Royalty, and that thus the reign of Thy peace may be established throughout the entire world. Amen.

(Plenary Indulgence once a day on the usual conditions.) (No. 254)

ACT OF CONSECRATION TO ST. ALPHONSUS LIGUORI

O most zealous Doctor of the Church, St. Alphonsus, I, though unworthy to be thy servant, yet encouraged by the goodness of thy heart, and by the great desire I have to please thee, come today, in presence of the Most Holy Trinity, of my Angel Guardian, and of the Court of Heaven, to choose thee for my Father, and, after Mary, my Patron and my Protector. I firmly promise to serve thee always, and to do all in my power to make others love thee also.

I entreat thee, then, my glorious Protector, by the love which thou bearest to Jesus and Mary, to receive me into the number of thy devoted children, and to protect me at all times. Obtain for me the grace to imitate thy virtues, and to advance in the true way of Christian perfection. Obtain for me especially, O my Father, detachment from creatures, a tender and constant devotion to the Blessed Sacrament and the Blessed Virgin Mary, the spirit of prayer, and an ardent zeal for the salvation of souls.

Accept this humble prayer as a sign of my consecration to thy service. Assist me during life, and especially at my death, so that having honored, and served thee on earth, I may deserve to share with thee the joys of Heaven for all eternity. Amen.

EJACULATION. My Protector, St. Alphonsus, in all my wants make me have recourse to Mary.

WAY OF THE CROSS INDULGENCES

All the faithful in the state of grace, who individually or collectively make the Way of the Cross with at least a contrite heart may gain the following indulgences:

1. A Plenary Indulgence as often as they make the Way of the Cross.

2. An *additional* Plenary Indulgence may be gained:

a.) Any day they make the Way of the Cross and receive Holy Communion;

b.) Or after making the Way of the Cross ten times, they receive Holy Communion within the month following.

3. If for some reasonable cause, the Way of the Cross is not completed, a partial Indulgence of ten years may be gained for each Station made. (Preces et Pia Opera No. 164)

The same indulgences are valid for the following:

a.) Those at sea, prisoners, sick persons and those who live in pagan countries, as well as those who are lawfully hindered from making the Stations in their ordinary form, provided that they hold in their hand a Crucifix blessed for this purpose by a Priest with the proper faculties, and recite with a contrite heart and devout sentiments twenty times Our Father, Hail Mary and Glory be, namely one for each Station, five in honor of the five Sacred Wounds of our Lord, and one for the intentions of the Sovereign Pontiff. If reasonably prevented from saying all, they are entitled to a partial indulgence of 10 years for each recitation of Our Father, Hail Mary and Glory be.

b.) The sick who on account of their condition cannot without serious inconvenience or difficulty perform the Way of the Cross in its ordinary form or in the shorter form described in paragraph *a)* may gain all the indulgences provided that they devoutly kiss, or at least fix their eyes upon a Crucifix, duly blessed for this purpose, which is held before them by a Priest or some other person, and recite, if possible, some short prayer or ejaculation in memory of the Passion and Death of our Lord Jesus Christ. (No. 164.)

His Holiness, Pope Pius XI, allowed those who cannot hold the crucifix in their hands because of manual labor or some other reasonable inconvenience the right to gain these indulgences as long as they have such a crucifix on their person while saying the prescribed prayers. (Nov. 9, 1933)

Redemptorist Fathers enjoy the privilege of blessing these Crucifixes.

Conditions to gain these Indulgences.

1. Movement from one Station to the other.
2. At each Station a brief meditation, according to one's ability, on the Passion of Our Lord and Saviour Jesus Christ.

No special form of prayer is required.

THE "STATIONS OF THE CROSS"

Prayers and Devotions Composed by
St. Alphonsus Liguori, about 1761.

Let each one make an Act of Contrition, and form the intention for the application of the Indulgences to be gained.

My Lord Jesus Christ, Thou hast made this journey to die for me with love unutterable, and I have so many times unworthily abandoned Thee; but now I love Thee with my whole heart, and because I love Thee I repent sincerely for having ever offended Thee. Pardon me, my God, and permit me to accompany Thee on this journey. Thou goest to die for love of me; I wish also, my beloved Redeemer, to die for love of Thee. My Jesus, I will live and die always united to Thee.

> Dear Jesus, Thou dost go to die
>   for very love of me;
> Ah, let me bear Thee company
>   I wish to die with Thee.

This stanza may be repeated while going from one Station to the other.

FIRST STATION.

Jesus is Condemned to Death.

V. We adore Thee, O Christ, and we bless Thee.

R. Because by Thy holy Cross Thou hast redeemed the world.

Consider how Jesus, after having been scourged and crowned with thorns, was unjustly condemned by Pilate to die on the Cross.

My adorable Jesus, it was not Pilate; no, it was my sins that condemned Thee to die. I beseech Thee, by the merits of this sorrowful journey to assist my soul in its journey towards eternity. I love Thee, my beloved Jesus; I love Thee more than myself; I repent with my whole heart of having offended Thee. Never permit me to separate myself from Thee again. Grant that I may love Thee always, and then do with me what Thou wilt.

Our Father.   Hail Mary.   Glory be to the Father.

My Jesus, have mercy on the souls in Purgatory.

Dear Jesus, etc.

SECOND STATION.

Jesus is Laden with the Cross.

V. We adore Thee, etc.

Consider how Jesus, in making this journey with the Cross on His shoulders, thought of us, and offered for us to His Father the death He was about to undergo.

My most beloved Jesus, I embrace all the tribulations Thou hast destined for me until death. I beseech Thee, by the merits of the pain Thou didst suffer in carrying Thy Cross, to give me the necessary help to carry mine with perfect patience and resignation. I love Thee, Jesus my love; I repent of having offended Thee. Never permit me to separate myself from Thee again. Grant that I may love Thee always, and then do with me what Thou wilt.

Our Father. Hail Mary. Glory be to the Father.
My Jesus, have mercy on the souls in Purgatory.
Dear Jesus, etc.

THIRD STATION.

Jesus Falls the First Time Under His Cross.

V. We adore Thee, etc.

Consider this first fall of Jesus under His Cross. His flesh was torn by the scourges, His head crowned with thorns, and He had lost a great quantity of blood. He was so weakened that He could scarcely walk, and yet He had to carry this great load upon His shoulders. The soldiers struck Him rudely, and thus He fell several times in His journey.

My Jesus, it is not the weight of the Cross, but of my sins, which has made Thee suffer so much pain. Ah! by the merits of this first fall, deliver me from the misfortune of falling into mortal sin. I love Thee, O my Jesus, with my whole heart; I repent of having offended Thee. Never permit me to offend Thee again. Grant that I may love Thee always, and then do with me what Thou wilt.

Our Father. Hail Mary. Glory be to the Father.
My Jesus, have mercy on the souls in Purgatory.
Dear Jesus, etc.

FOURTH STATION.

Jesus Meets His Afflicted Mother

V. We adore Thee, etc.
Consider the meeting of the Son and the Mother, which took place on this journey. Jesus and Mary looked at each other, and their looks became as so many arrows to wound those hearts which loved each other so tenderly.

My most loving Jesus, by the sorrow that Thou didst experience in this meeting, grant me the grace of a truly devoted love for Thy most holy

Mother. And thou, my Queen, who wast overwhelmed with sorrow, obtain for me, by thy intercession, a continual and tender remembrance of the passion of thy Son. I love Thee, Jesus my love; I repent of having offended Thee. Never permit me to offend Thee again. Grant that I may love Thee, and then do with me what Thou wilt.

Our Father. Hail Mary. Glory be to the Father.
My Jesus, have mercy on the souls in Purgatory.
Dear Jesus, etc.

FIFTH STATION.

The Cyrenian Helps Jesus to Carry His Cross.

V. We adore Thee, etc.
Consider how the Jews, seeing that at each step, Jesus, from weakness, was on the point of expiring, and fearing that He would die on the way, when they wished Him to die the ignominious death of the Cross, constrained Simon, the Cyrenian, to carry the Cross behind our Lord.

My most beloved Jesus, I will not

refuse the Cross as the Cyrenian did; I accept it—I embrace it. It accept in particular the death Thou hast destined for me, with all the pains which may accompany it; I unite it to Thy death—I offer it to Thee. Thou hast died for love of me; I will die for love of Thee, and to please Thee. Help me by Thy grace. I love Thee, Jesus my love; I repent of having offended Thee. Never permit me to offend Thee again. Grant that I may love Thee, and then do with me what Thou wilt.

Our Father. Hail Mary. Glory be to the Father.

My Jesus, have mercy on the souls in Purgatory.

Dear Jesus, etc.

SIXTH STATION.

Veronica Wipes the Face of Jesus

V. We adore Thee, etc.

Consider how the holy woman named Veronica, seeing Jesus so afflicted, and His face bathed in sweat and blood, presented Him with a towel, with which He wiped His adorable face, leaving on it the impression of His holy countenance.

My most beloved Jesus, Thy face was beautiful before, but in this journey it has lost all its beauty, and wounds and blood have disfigured it. Alas! my soul also was once beautiful, when it received Thy grace in Baptism; but I have disfigured it since by my sins. Thou alone, my Redeemer, canst restore it to its former beauty. Do this by Thy Passion, and then do with me what Thou wilt.

Our Father. Hail Mary. Glory be to the Father.

My Jesus, have mercy on the souls in Purgatory.

Dear Jesus, etc.

SEVENTH STATION.

Jesus Falls the Second Time.

V. We adore Thee, etc.

Consider the second fall of Jesus under the Cross—a fall which renews the pain of all the wounds of the head and members of our afflicted Lord.

My most gentle Jesus, how many times Thou hast pardoned me, and how many times have I fallen again, and begun again to offend Thee! Oh! by the merits of this new fall, give me the necessary helps to persevere in Thy grace until death. Grant that in all temptations which assail me, I may always commend myself to Thee. I love Thee, Jesus my love, with my whole heart; I repent of having offended Thee. Never permit me to offend Thee again. Grant that I may love Thee always, and then do with me what Thou wilt.

Our Father. Hail Mary. Glory be to the Father.
My Jesus, have mercy on the souls in Purgatory.
Dear Jesus, etc.

EIGHTH STATION.

Jesus Speaks to the Women of Jerusalem.

V. We adore Thee, etc.
Consider how those women wept with compassion at seeing Jesus in such a pitiable state, streaming with Blood, as He walked along. But Jesus said to them: *Weep not for Me, but for your children.*

My Jesus, laden with sorrows, I weep for the offences I have committed against Thee, because of the pains they have deserved, and still more because of the displeasure they have caused Thee, Who hast loved me so much. It is Thy love more than the fear of hell, which causes me to weep for my sins. My Jesus, I love Thee more than myself; I repent of having offended Thee. Never permit me to offend Thee again. Grant that I may love Thee always, and then do with me what Thou wilt.

Our Father. Hail Mary. Glory be to the Father.
My Jesus, have mercy on the souls in Purgatory.
Dear Jesus, etc.

NINTH STATION.
Jesus Falls the Third Time.

V. We adore Thee, etc.
Consider the third fall of Jesus Christ. His weakness was extreme, and the cruelty of His executioners excessive, who tried to hasten His steps when He had scarcely strength to move.

Ah, my outraged Jesus, by the merits of the weakness Thou didst suffer in going to Calvary, give me strength sufficient to conquer all human respect, and all my wicked passions, which have led me to despise Thy friendship. I love Thee, Jesus my love, with my whole heart; I repent of having offended Thee. Never permit me to offend Thee again. Grant that I may love Thee always, and then do with me what Thou wilt.

Our Father. Hail Mary. Glory be to the Father.
My Jesus, have mercy on the souls in Purgatory.
Dear Jesus, etc.

TENTH STATION.
Jesus is Stripped of His Garments.

V. We adore Thee, etc.
Consider the violence with which the executioners stripped Jesus. His inner garments adhered to His torn flesh, and they dragged them off so roughly that the skin came with them. Compassionate your Saviour thus cruelly treated, and say to Him:

My innocent Jesus, by the merits of

the torments Thou has felt, help me to strip myself of all affection to things of earth, in order that I may place all my love in Thee, Who art so worthy of my love. I love Thee, O Jesus, with my whole heart: I repent of having offended Thee. Never permit me to offend Thee again. Grant That I may love Thee always, and then do with me what Thou wilt.

Our Father. Hail Mary. Glory be to the Father.
My Jesus, have mercy on the souls in Purgatory.
Dear Jesus, etc.

ELEVENTH STATION.
Jesus is Nailed to the Cross.

V. We adore Thee, etc.
Consider how Jesus, after being thrown on the Cross, extended His hands, and offered to His Eternal Father the sacrifice of His life for our salvation. These barbarians fastened Him with nails, and then, raising the Cross, leave Him to die with anguish on this infamous gibbet.

My Jesus! loaded with contempt, nail my heart to Thy feet, that it may ever remain there, to love Thee, and never quit Thee again. I love Thee more than myself; I repent of having offended Thee. Never permit me to offend Thee again. Grant that I may love Thee always, and then do with me what Thou wilt.

Our Father. Hail Mary. Glory be to the Father.
My Jesus, have mercy on the souls in Purgatory.
Dear Jesus, etc.

TWELFTH STATION.

Jesus Dies on the Cross.

V. We adore Thee, etc.
Consider how thy Jesus, after three hours agony on the Cross, consumed at length with anguish, abandons Himself to the weight of His body, bows His head, and dies.

O my dying Jesus, I kiss devoutly the Cross on which Thou didst die for love of me. I have merited by my sins to die a miserable death, but Thy death is my hope. Ah, by the merits of Thy death, give me grace to die embracing Thy feet, and burning with love for Thee. I yield my soul into Thy hands. I love Thee with my whole heart; I repent of having offended Thee. Never permit me to offend Thee again. Grant that I may love Thee always, and then do with me what Thou wilt.

Our Father. Hail Mary. Glory be to the Father.

My Jesus, have mercy on the souls in Purgatory.

Dear Jesus, Thou didst go to die
  For very love of me;
Ah, let me bear Thee company;
  I wish to die with Thee.

THIRTEENTH STATION.

Jesus is Taken Down from the Cross.

V. We adore Thee, etc.

Consider how, after the death of our Lord, two of His disciples, Joseph and Nicodemus, took Him down from the Cross, and placed Him in the arms of His afflicted Mother, who received Him with unutterable tenderness, and pressed Him to her bosom.

O Mother of Sorrows, for the love of this Son, accept me for thy servant, and pray to Him for me. And Thou, my Redeemer, since Thou hast died for me, permit me to love Thee; for I wish but Thee and nothing more. I love Thee, my Jesus, and I repent of having offended Thee. Never permit me to offend Thee again. Grant that I may love Thee always, and then do with me what Thou wilt.

Our Father. Hail Mary. Glory be to the Father.
My Jesus, have mercy on the souls in Purgatory.
Dear Jesus, etc.

FOURTEENTH STATION.

Jesus is Placed in the Sepulchre.

V. We adore Thee, etc.
Consider how the disciples carried the body of Jesus to bury it, accompanied by His Holy Mother, who arranged it in the sepulchre with her own hands. They then closed the tomb, and all withdrew.

Ah, my buried Jesus, I kiss the stone that encloses Thee. But Thou didst rise again the third day. I beseech Thee by Thy resurrection, make me rise glorious with Thee at the last day, to be always united with Thee in Heaven, to praise Thee and love Thee for ever. I love Thee, and I repent of having offended Thee. Never permit me to offend Thee again. Grant that I may love Thee, and then do with me what Thou wilt.

Our Father.   Hail Mary.   Glory be to the Father.

My Jesus, have mercy on the souls in Purgatory.

Dear Jesus, etc.

STABAT MATER.

(Composed by Jacopone da Todi, who died 1306)

1. At the Cross her station keeping,
    Stood the mournful Mother weeping,
      Close to Jesus to the last:
    Through her heart His sorrow sharing,
    All His bitter anguish bearing,
      Now at length the sword had passed.

2. Oh, how sad and sore-distressed
Was that Mother highly blest
   Of the sole begotten One!
Christ above in torment hangs;
She beneath beholds the pangs
   Of her dying, glorious Son.

3. Is there one who would not weep
Whelmed in miseries so deep
   Christ's dear Mother to behold?
Can the human heart refrain
From partaking in her pain,—
   In that Mother's pain untold?

4. Bruised, derided, cursed, defiled,
She beheld her tender Child,
   All with bloody scourges rent:
For the sins of His own nation
Saw Him hang in desolation,
   Till His spirit forth He sent.

5. O thou Mother, fount of love!
Touch my spirit from above,
   Make my heart with thine accord;
Make me feel as thou hast felt,
Make my soul to glow and melt
   With the love of Christ, my Lord.

6. Holy Mother, pierce me through,
In my heart each wound renew
   Of my Saviour crucified.

Let me share with thee His pain,
Who for all my sins was slain,
  Who for me in torments died.

7. Let me mingle tears with thee,
Mourning Him Who mourned for me,
  All the days that I may live;
By the Cross with thee to stay,
There with thee to weep and pray,
  Is all I ask of thee to give.

8. Virgin of all virgins best!
Listen to my fond request:
  Let me share thy grief divine;
Let me to my latest breath,
In my body bear the death
  Of that dying Son of thine.

9. Wounded with His every wound,
Steep my soul till it has swooned,
  In His very Blood away;
Be to me, O Virgin, nigh,
Lest in flames I burn and die
  In His awful judgment-day.

10. Christ, when Thou shalt call me hence,
Be Thy Mother my defence,
  Be Thy Cross my victory;
While my body here decays,
May my soul Thy goodness praise
  Safe in Paradise with Thee.

*Seven years' indulgence. (No. 344)

The Plenary Indulgence for the hour of death attached to a Crucifix may be gained, without the assistance of a Priest, under the following conditions:

1. The reception of the Sacraments. If unable to receive them, the dying person must be contrite for all sins committed.

2. The holy name of Jesus must be pronounced orally, if possible, or else at least in one's heart.

3. The Crucifix must be near the dying, or at least be near the bed, although it is not necessary that he sees it, when there is question of Papal indulgences. But the so-called Crucifixes for the dying must be either kissed or touched by the dying.

4. Death must be accepted with resignation to the holy will of God.

The Redemptorist Fathers have the faculty to indulgence Crucifixes for the above-mentioned purposes, and attach the Plenary Indulgence for the hour of death. This indulgence remains even though the Crucifix passes over into the possession of another, or is used by another, and can be gained by any one who uses the Crucifix, no matter, whether he is the owner or not.

The most important condition for gaining any indulgence, whether partial or plenary, is to have a true hatred of all sins, even venial sin.

THE PROTESTATION FOR A HAPPY DEATH.

(By St. Alphonsus.)

My God, prostrate in Thy presence, I adore Thee; and I intend to make the following protestation, is if I were on the point of passing from this life into eternity.

My Lord, because Thou art the infallible Truth, and hast revealed it to the Holy Church, I believe in the mystery of the most Holy Trinity, Father, Son, and Holy Ghost; three Persons, but only one God; Who for all eternity rewards the just in Heaven, and punishes the wicked in hell. I believe that the Second Person, that is, the Son of God, became Man, and died for the salvation of mankind; and I believe all that the Holy Church believes. I thank Thee for having made me a Christian, and I protest that I will live and die in this holy Faith.

My God, my Hope, trusting in

Thy promises, I hope from Thy mercy, not through my own merits, but through the merits of Jesus Christ, for the pardon of my sins, perseverance in Thy grace, and, after this miserable life, the glory of Paradise. And should the devil at death tempt me to despair at the sight of my sins, I protest that I will always hope in Thee, O Lord, and that I desire to die in the loving arms of Thy goodness.

O God, worthy of infinite love, I love Thee with my whole heart, more than I love myself; and I protest that I desire to die making an act of love that I may thus continue to love Thee eternally in Heaven which, for this end, I desire and ask of Thee. And if hitherto, O Lord, instead of loving Thee, I have despised Thy infinite goodness, I repent of it with all my heart, and I protest that I wish to die, always weeping over and detesting the offences I have committed against Thee. I purpose for the future rather to die than ever to sin again; and for the love of Thee I pardon all who have offended me.

O my God, I accept death, and all the sufferings which will accompany it; I unite it with the sufferings and death of Jesus Christ, and offer it in acknowledgment of Thy supreme dominion, and in satisfaction for my sins. Do Thou, O Lord, accept of this sacrifice which I make of my life, for the love of that great Sacrifice which Thy Divine Son made of Himself upon the altar of the Cross. I resign myself entirely to Thy Divine will, as though I were now on my death-bed, and protest that I wish to die, saying: O Lord, always Thy will be done.

Most holy Virgin, my Advocate and my Mother Mary, thou art and wilt always be, after God, my hope and my consolation at the hour of death. From this moment I have recourse to thee, and beg of thee to assist me in that passage. O my dear Queen, do not abandon me in that last moment! Come then to take my soul and present it to thy Son. Henceforward I shall expect thee; and I hope to die under thy mantle, and clinging to thy feet. My Protector, St. Joseph, St. Michael Archangel, my Angel Guardian, my Holy Patrons, do you all assist me in that last combat with hell.

And Thou, my Crucified Love, Thou my Jesus, Who wert pleased to choose for Thyself so bitter a death to obtain for me a good death, remember at that hour that I am one of those dear sheep Thou didst purchase with Thy Blood. Thou, when all the world shall have forsaken me, and not one shall be able to assist me, canst alone console me and save me, do Thou make me worthy to receive Thee in the Viaticum, and suffer me not to lose Thee forever, and to be banished forever to a distance from

Thee. No, my beloved Saviour, receive me then into Thy sacred Wounds, for I now embrace Thee. At my last breath I intend to breathe forth my soul into the loving wound in Thy side, saying now, for that moment: Jesus and Mary, I give you my heart and my soul.

O happy suffering, to suffer for God! happy death, to die in the Lord!

I embrace Thee now, my good Redeemer, that I may die in Thy embraces. If, O my soul, Mary assists you at your departure, and Jesus receives your last breath, it will not be death, but a sweet repose.

Then it will not be death, but ineffable rest
  That will close, in the end, on these earth-wearied eyes.
When my forehead by Mary is soothingly pressed,
  And Jesus receives my last penitent sighs.

(No. 591.)

PRAYER FOR A GOOD DEATH.

O Lord Jesus, God of goodness and Father of mercies, I draw nigh to

Thee with a contrite and humble heart; to Thee I recommend the last hour of my life, and that judgment which awaits me afterwards,

Merciful Jesus, have mercy on me.

When my feet, benumbed with death, shall admonish me that my course in this life is drawing to an end,

Merciful Jesus, have mercy on me.

When my hands, cold and trembling, shall no longer be able to clasp the Crucifix, and shall let it fall against my will on my bed of suffering,

Merciful Jesus, have mercy on me.

When my eyes, dim with trouble at the approach of death, shall fix themselves on Thee, my last and only support,

Merciful Jesus, have mercy on me.

When my lips, cold and trembling, shall pronounce for the last time Thy adorable Name.

Merciful Jesus, have mercy on me.

When my face, pale and livid, shall inspire the beholders with pity and dismay; when my hair, bathed in the sweat of death, and stiffening on my head, shall forebode my approaching end,

Merciful Jesus, have mercy on me.

When my ears, soon to be for ever shut to the discourse of men, shall be open to the irrevocable decree which is to fix my doom for all eternity,

Merciful Jesus, have mercy on me.

When my imagination, agitated by dreadful spectres, shall be sunk in an abyss of anguish; when my soul, affrighted with the sight of my iniquities and the terrors of Thy judgment, shall have to fight against the angel of darkness, who will endeavor to conceal from my eyes Thy mercies, and to plunge me into despair,

Merciful Jesus, have mercy on me.

When my poor heart, oppressed with suffering and exhausted by its continual struggles with the enemies of its salvation, shall feel the pangs of death,

Merciful Jesus, have mercy on me.

When the last tear, the forerunner of my dissolution, shall drop from my eyes, receive it as a sacrifice of expiation for my sins; grant that I may expire the victim of penance; and then in that dreadful moment,

Merciful Jesus, have mercy on me.

When my friends and relations, encircling my bed, shall be moved with compassion for me, and invoke Thy clemency in my behalf,

Merciful Jesus, have mercy on me.

When I shall have lost the use of my senses; when the world shall have vanished from my sight; when my agonizing soul shall feel the sorrows of death,

Merciful Jesus, have mercy on me.

When my soul, trembling on my lips, shall bid adieu to the world, and leave my body lifeless, pale and cold, receive this separation as a homage in that last moment of my mortal life,

Merciful Jesus, have mercy on me:

When at length my soul, admitted to Thy presence, shall first behold the splendor of Thy Majesty, reject it not, but receive me into Thy bosom, where I may for ever sing Thy praises,

Merciful Jesus, have mercy on me.

Let us Pray.

O God, Who hast doomed all men to die, but hast concealed from all the hour of their death, grant that I may pass my days in the practice of holiness and justice, and that I may be made worthy to quit this world, in the embrace of Thy love. Through the merits of our Lord Jesus Christ, Who liveth and reigneth with Thee in the unity of the Holy Spirit. Amen.

ETERNITY!

> "With desolation is all the land made desolate because there is none that considereth in his heart."—Jeremiah xii, 11.

Oh, how long, how immense, how happy, or how miserable will be

ETERNITY!

Mortal men, endowed with immortal souls! study, meditate, and weigh well this great word:

ETERNITY!

Oh, Eternity, how far thou art from the thoughts of men! how seldom do men reflect on thee,

ETERNITY!

Oh, Eternity! what shall I say of thee? how shall I say it? who can fully understand the meaning of this word,

ETERNITY!

I think of a thousand years—of a hundred times a thousand years—of a hundred millions of times a thousand years—I fancy to myself as many millions of years as there are leaves in the forest, blades of grass on the earth, grains of sand on the sea-shore, drops of water in the ocean, atoms in the air, and stars in the firmament, and still I have not yet begun to express the meaning of this word:

ETERNITY!

Oh, Eternity of bliss! who would not long for thee! Oh, Eternity of woe! who would not fear thee! What would I say! I cannot express, I cannot even conceive it. As long as God shall be God, Heaven will last. As long as God shall be God, hell will endure. But how long will that be? for ever and for ever, for

ETERNITY!

Pleasures pass away; the punishments of pleasure will be eternal. Afflictions pass away; their recompense will last for all Eternity. Choose, then, the joys of a moment, and the sufferings of a moment and the joys of Eternity. Eternity depends on death, death on life, life on a moment, and on that moment depends:

ETERNITY!

Prayer.

O my God, I present myself before Thee, with a heartfelt sorrow for my sins. I humbly adore Thee; I believe in Thee and Thy Holy Catholic Church, and in Eternity. I hope in Thee, and, through Thy goodness, I hope for a happy Eternity. I love Thee with my whole heart, and for Eternity. I submit myself to whatever Thou shalt ordain concerning me; "here cut, here burn, but spare me in Eternity." Grant me, O Almighty and merciful God, the grace I stand in need of to serve Thee faithfully during life, and to possess Thee in Eternity. Through Christ, our Lord. Amen.

"In Thee, O Lord, have I hoped; let me never be confounded."

Sorrowful Mother Mary, pray for me now and at the hour of my death. Amen.

PRAYER OF A SOUL IN DESOLATION.

"My Father, if it be possible, let this chalice pass from Me; nevertheless not as I will, but as Thou wilt." (Matth. xxvi, 39.)

I love Thee, though I seem
An enemy in Thy sight;
Repel me as Thou wilt,
I will ever follow Thee.

"What have I in Heaven, and besides Thee what do I desire upon earth? Thou art the God of my heart, and the God that is my portion forever." (Ps. lxxii. 25, 26.)

My God, my God, all mine Thou art;
Myself I give Thee, all my heart;
For Thee, and Thee alone, I sigh.

EXPLANATION OF A NOVENA.

A "Novena" consists of acts of devotion, performed on nine consecutive days, to obtain a particular grace of either spiritual or temporal nature. These acts of devotion may consist of vocal prayers (for instance, nine "Hail Marys," followed by a "Hail, Holy Queen," or any other short prayer, or nine "Glory be to the Father," or a fixed number of ejaculatory prayers whilst at work, etc.); reception of the holy sacraments; acts of mortification (for example to refrain from unnecessary talk, to abstain from a particular kind of food we have a craving for, to break off sleep, and to spend this time in a pious manner, not to take a very comfortable posture while at prayer, etc.)

A person may choose the acts of devotion for himself, or better still, have them determined by his spiritual director. Particular care should be taken to avoid even the least voluntary venial sin and fault.

By a Novena pious Catholics prepare themselves for the feasts of our Lord, the Blessed Virgin, or a particular saint; or pay honor to a special mystery of our holy religion.

The first Novena was made by the Blessed Virgin and the Apostles, at the command of our Lord Himself. It lasted from the Ascension of Christ into Heaven until the descent of the Holy Ghost on the feast of Pentecost.

NOVENA FOR THE HOLY SOULS IN PURGATORY.

(By St. Alphonsus de Liguori.)

Let us commend to Jesus Christ and His holy Mother the souls in Purgatory, in particular those of our relatives, benefactors, friends, and enemies; especially those for whom we are bound to pray; and let us offer the following considerations and prayers for them, pondering over the great sufferings which these spouses of Christ endure.

FIRST DAY.

Manifold are the sufferings which those blessed souls must endure, but the greatest of all is the reflection that their sins in life are the cause of their present torments.

Prayer.

O Jesus, my Saviour, I have so often deserved to be cast into hell; how great were my suffering if I were now cast away and obliged to think that I, myself, had caused my damnation! I thank Thee for the patience with which Thou hast endured me. My God, I love Thee above all things and I am heartily sorry for having offended Thee because Thou art infinite goodness. I will rather die than offend Thee again. Grant me the grace of perseverance; have pity on me, and at the same time on those blessed souls suffering in Purgatory. Mary, Mother of God, come to their assistance with thy powerful intercession.

Our Father. Hail Mary.

On Thy spouses have compassion,
On these suffering children Thine;
Make these holy souls partakers
Of Thy happiness Divine.

PRAYER TO OUR SUFFERING SAVIOUR FOR THE SOULS IN PURGATORY.

To be repeated every day during the Novena.

V. O most sweet Jesus, through the bloody sweat which Thou didst suffer in the Garden of Gethsemani, have mercy on these blessed souls.

R. Have mercy on them, O Lord, have mercy on them.

V. O most sweet Jesus, through the pains which Thou didst suffer during Thy most cruel scourging, have mercy on them.

R. Have mercy on them, O Lord.

V. O most sweet Jesus, through the pains which Thou didst suffer in Thy most painful crowning with thorns, have mercy on them.

R. Have mercy on them, etc.

V. O most sweet Jesus, through the pains which Thou didst suffer in carrying Thy Cross to Calvary, have mercy on them.

R. Have mercy on them, etc.

V. O most sweet Jesus, through the pains which Thou didst suffer during Thy most cruel Crucifixion, have mercy on them.

R. Have mercy on them, etc.

V. O most sweet Jesus, through the pains which Thou didst suffer in Thy most bitter agony on the Cross, have mercy on them.

R. Have mercy on them, etc.

V. O most sweet Jesus, through the immense pain which Thou didst suffer in breathing forth Thy blessed soul, have mercy on them.

R. Have mercy on them, etc.

(Here recommend yourself to the souls in Purgatory, and mention the favor you wish to obtain by this Novena.)

Blessed souls, we have prayed for you; we entreat you, who are so dear to God, and who are secure of never losing Him, to pray for us miserable sinners, who are in danger of being damned, and of losing God forever. Amen.

SECOND DAY.

The second pain which causes these holy souls much suffering, is the time lost in life, when they might have gained merits for Heaven; and the thought, that they are unable to repair this loss, because the time of life and merit is passed.

Prayer.

Woe to me, unhappy being, so many years have I already spent on earth, and have earned naught but hell! I give Thee thanks, O Lord, for granting me time even now to atone for my sins. My good God, I am heartily sorry for having offended Thee. Send me Thy assistance, that I may apply the time yet remaining to me for Thy love and service; have compassion on me, and, at the same time, on the holy souls suffering in Purgatory. O Mary, Mother of God, come to their assistance with thy powerful intercession.

"Our Father," "Hail Mary," "On Thy spouses," etc. "O most sweet Jesus," etc.

THIRD DAY.

Another great pain of the holy souls is caused by the hideous vision of their guilt, for which they now suffer. In this life the hideousness of sin is not seen as in the life to come; and this one of the greatest sufferings of Purgatory.

Prayer.

O my God! because Thou art infinite goodness, I love Thee above all things, and repent with my whole heart of my offences against Thee. Grant me the grace of holy perseverance. Have compassion on me, and, at the same time, on the holy souls suffering in Purgatory. And thou, Mary, Mother of God, come to their assistance with thy powerful intercession.

"Our Father," "Hail Mary," "On Thy spouses," etc. "O most sweet Jesus," etc.

FOURTH DAY.

The pain that still more afflicts these holy souls, the spouses of Jesus, is the thought of having, during life, displeased by their sins that God Whom they so ardently love. Some penitents have felt so much pain and sorrow in thinking of having, by their sins, offended so good a God, that they died of grief. The souls in Purgatory understand far better than we do, the claims that God has to our love; they love Him with all their strength. Hence, at the thought of having offended Him during life, they experience pain that surpasses all other pain.

Prayer.

O my God! because Thou art infinite goodness, I am sorry with my whole heart for having offended Thee. I promise to die rather than ever offend Thee more. Give me holy perservance; have pity on me, and have pity on those holy souls that burn in the cleansing fire, and love Thee with all their hearts. O Mary, Mother of God, assist them by thy powerful prayers.

"Our Father," "Hail Mary," "On Thy spouses," etc. "O most sweet Jesus," etc.

FIFTH DAY.

Another great suffering is caused these holy souls by the ignorance of the time of their deliverance. They are certain of being one day released, yet the uncertainty of the time when their purgatorial term will have ended, gives them great pain.

Prayer.

Woe to me, unhappy being, if Thou, O Lord, hadst cast me into hell; for from that dungeon of eternal pain there is no deliverance. I love Thee above all things, O infinite God, and I am sincerely sorry for having ever offended Thee again. Grant me the grace of holy perseverance. Have compassion on me, and, at the same time, on the holy souls suffering in Purgatory. O Mary, Mother of God, come to their assistance with thy powerful intercession.

"Our Father," "Hail Mary," "On Thy spouses," etc. "O most sweet Jesus," etc.

SIXTH DAY.

The holy souls are, indeed, comforted by the recollection of the passion of Jesus Christ, and the Holy Sacrament of the Altar, since they know they are saved by the passion of Jesus Christ, and have received, and still receive, so much consolation from Holy Masses and Holy Communions. Nevertheless, they are greatly pained by the recollection of their ingratitude for these two great gifts of the love of Jesus Christ.

Prayer.

O my Divine Redeemer, Thou didst die for me on the Cross, and hast so often united Thyself with me in Holy Communion, and I have repaid Thee only with ingratitude. Now, however, I love Thee above all things, O supreme God; and I am more grieved at my offences against Thee than at any other evil. I will rather die than offend Thee again. Grant me the grace of holy perservance. Have compassion on me, and, at the same time, on the holy souls suffering in Purgatory. Mary, Mother of God, come to their aid with thy powerful intercession.

"Our Father," "Hail Mary," "On Thy spouses," etc. "O most sweet Jesus," etc.

SEVENTH DAY.

A further great sorrow of these holy souls consists in their ardent desire for the beatific vision. Slowly and painfully the moments of their purgatorial imprisonment pass by; for, they love God deeply, and desire to be delivered from their sad prison in order to praise Him forever.

Prayer.

O God, Father of Mercy, satisfy

this their ardent desire! Send them Thy holy Angel to announce to them that Thou, Their Father, art now reconciled with them through the suffering and death of Jesus, and that the moment of their deliverance has arrived.

"Our Father," "Hail Mary," "On Thy spouses," etc. "O most sweet Jesus," etc.

EIGHTH DAY.

Another bitter sorrow of these souls is caused by the reflection that God had distinguished them by so many graces not granted to others, and that they compelled Him, by their sins, to condemn them to these sufferings, and that they had deserved hell, and were pardoned and saved only by the mercy of God.

Prayer.

O my God! I also am one of these ungrateful beings, having received so much grace, and yet despised Thy love, and deserved to be cast by Thee into hell. But Thy infinite goodness has spared me until now. Therefore, I now love Thee above all things, and I am heartily sorry for having offended Thee. I will rather die than ever again offend Thee. Grant me the grace of holy perseverance. Have compassion on me and, at the same time, on the holy souls suffering in Purgatory. Mary, Mother of God, come to their aid with thy powerful intercession.

"Our Father," "Hail Mary," "On Thy spouses," etc. "O most sweet Jesus," etc.

NINTH DAY.

Great are all the sufferings of the holy souls; the fire, the grief, the darkness, the uncertainty of the time of their deliverance from prison; but the greatest of all these sorrows is this, that these holy souls are separated from their divine Spouse, and deprived of His beatific vision.

Prayer.

O my God! how was it possible that I, for so many years, have borne tranquilly the separation from Thee and Thy holy grace! O infinite Goodness, how long-suffering hast Thou shown Thyself to me! Henceforth, I shall love Thee above all things. I am deeply sorry for having offended Thee; I promise rather to die than to again offend Thee. Grant me the grace of holy perseverance, and do not permit that I should ever again fall into sin.

Have compassion on the holy souls suffering in Purgatory. I pray Thee, moderate their sufferings; shorten the time of their misery; call them soon unto Thee in Heaven, that they may behold Thee face to face, and forever love Thee.

Mary, Mother of Mercy, come to their aid with thy powerful intercession, and pray for us also who are still in danger of eternal damnation.

"Our Father," "Hail Mary," "On Thy spouses," etc. "O most sweet Jesus," etc.

De Profundis.
Ps. 129.

Out of the depths I have cried to Thee, O Lord! Lord hear my voice.

Let Thine ears be attentive to the voice of my supplication.

If Thou, O Lord, shalt mark our iniquities; O Lord, who shall stand it?

For with Thee there is merciful forgiveness; and by reason of Thy law I have waited for Thee, O Lord.

My soul hath relied on His word; my soul hath hoped in the Lord.

From the morning watch even unto night, let Israel hope in the Lord.

Because with the Lord there is mercy; and with Him plenteous redemption.

And He shall redeem Israel from all his iniquities.

Eternal rest grant unto them, O Lord, and let perpetual light shine upon them; may they rest in peace. Amen.

*Three years' indulgence. Plenary indulgence under the usual conditions, once a month. (No. 539)

AN ACT OF CONSECRATION TO THE HOLY FAMILY.

To be recited by Christian families who consecrate themselves to the Holy Family.

"O Jesus, our most loving Saviour! Thou Who wast sent down from Heaven to enlighten the world by Thy teaching and example, and Who didst will to pass the greater part of Thy holy life in lowliness at Thy home in Nazareth, subject to Mary and Joseph, and thereby didst hallow the household which was to be the pattern for all Christian families, do Thou in Thy goodness receive our household which this day consecrates itself to Thee. Protect and guard us, strengthen us in Thy holy fear, establish in our hearts the peace and concord of Christian Charity, so that each one of us becoming like to the divine model of Thy family, may be sharers of eternal joy."

"O Mary, most loving Mother of Jesus Christ, our Mother, through thy love and mercy intercede, that Jesus receive this act of Consecration, and pour out upon us His graces and blessings."

"O Joseph, most holy Guardian of Jesus and Mary, help us by thy prayers in all our necessities, both of body and soul; that together with the Blessed Virgin Mary and thyself we shall praise and thank Jesus Christ, our Divine Redeemer."

A Prayer To Be Said Every Day Before a Picture of the Holy Family.

"O most loving Jesus, Who didst hallow by Thy surpassing virtues and the example of Thy home-life, the household Thou didst choose to live in whilst upon earth, mercifully look down upon this family, whose members, humbly prostrate before Thee, implore Thy protection. Remember that we are Thine, bound and consecrated to Thee by a special devotion. Protect us in Thy mercy, deliver us from danger, help us in our necessities and impart to us strength to persevere always in the imitation of Thy Holy Family, so that by serving Thee and loving Thee faithfully during this mortal life, we may at length give Thee eternal praise in Heaven.

O Mary, dearest Mother, we implore thy assistance, knowing that thy Divine Son will hearken to thy petitions.

And do thou, most glorious Patriarch, St. Joseph, help us with thy powerful patronage, and place our petitions in Mary's hands, that she may offer them to Jesus Christ."

Jesus, Mary, Joseph, I give you my heart and my soul.

Jesus, Mary, Joseph, assist me in my last agony.

Jesus, Mary, Joseph, may I breathe forth my soul in peace with you.

*Seven years' indulgence for each invocation. (No. 589)

DEVOTION TO OUR LADY OF PERPETUAL HELP.

The miraculous Picture of *Our Lady of Perpetual Help*, which had been an object of devotion in the Island of Crete, was brought from thence to Rome, where for three centuries, it was venerated in the Church of St. Matthew. This Church was destroyed during the French Revolution, and the Picture was forgotten for 60 years, until, on the 26th of April, 1866, it was, by order of the Holy

Father, Pius IX., again exposed to public veneration in the Church of the Redemptorist Fathers, dedicated to St. Alphonsus Maria de Liguori.

From that day the popular devotion towards the holy Picture has spread all over the world: and by means of it the Blessed Virgin has bestowed many graces on her devout clients. The Chapter of St. Peter's crowned the holy Image with a golden diadem, on the 23rd of June, 1867.

Triduo.

FIRST DAY.

Behold at thy feet, *O Mother of Perpetual Help!* a miserable sinner who has recourse to thee, and confides in thee. O Mother of Mercy, have pity on me. I hear thee called by all the refuge and the hope of sinners; be then my refuge and my hope. Assist me for the love of Jesus Christ; stretch forth thy hand to a miserable wretch, who has fallen and who recommends himself to thee, and who consecrates himself to be thy servant forever. I bless and thank Almighty God, Who, by His mercy has given me this confidence in thee, which I hold to be a pledge of my eternal salvation. It is true, that in past times I have miserably fallen into sin, because I had not recourse to thee. I know that with thy help I will be able to conquer. I know, too, that thou wilt assist me if I recommend myself to thee; but I fear that in the time of danger I may neglect to call on thee, and thus lose my soul. The grace, therefore, which I ask of thee, and for which I beg with all the fervor of my soul, is, that in all the attacks of hell, I may ever have recourse to thee, and say to thee: O Mary, help me; *O Mother of Perpetual Help*, never permit me to lose my God.

Five Hail Marys.

V. Pray for us, O holy Mother of God.

R. That we may be made worthy of the promises of Christ.

Let us pray.

O Lord Jesus Christ, Who hast given us Thine own Mother Mary, whose glorious image we venerate, to be our Mother ever ready to come to our help; grant, we beseech Thee, that we, unceasingly imploring her motherly help, may merit always to experience the fruit of Thy Redemption, Who livest and reignest world without end. Amen.

SECOND DAY.

O Mother of Perpetual Help! grant that I may ever invoke thy most powerful name, which is the safeguard of the living and the salvation of the dying. O purest Mary, O sweetest Mary, let thy name be henceforth the breath of my life. Do not hesitate, O Blessed Lady, to help me whenever I call on thee, to assist me; for in every temptation which will assail me, in all the necessities which may afflict me, I will never cease to call on thee by often repeating: O Mary! O Mary! O what consolation, what sweetness and confidence, and what emotion does not my soul experience when I utter thy name, or only think of thee! I thank Almighty God for having given thee, on my account, so sweet, so powerful, so lovely a name. But I will not be content with the mere invocation of thy name. I will call on thee, burning with love for thee, and beg that my love for thee may prompt me constantly to salute thee: *O Mother of Perpetual Help!*

5 Hail Marys, and prayer as above.

THIRD DAY.

O Mother of Perpetual Help! thou art the dispenser of all those gifts which God grants to us miserable sinners, and for this end He has made thee so powerful, so rich, and so bountiful in order that thou mayest succor us in our misery. Thou art the advocate of those sinners who are more miserable and abandoned than the rest, and who have recourse to thee. Into thy hands I place my eternal salvation, and to thee I consign my soul. I wish to be numbered among thy most devoted servants; take me under thy protection, and it is enough for me. For if thou protect me, I fear nothing, neither from my sins, because thou wilt obtain for me the pardon of them; nor from the devils, because thou art more powerful than all hell together; nor even from Jesus Christ, my Judge Himself, because by one prayer from thee He will be appeased. But one thing I fear, that in the hour of temptation I may, from extreme negligence, fail to have recourse to thee, and thus perish miserably. Obtain for me, therefore, the pardon of my sins, final perseverance, and the priceless gift to love Jesus Christ, and ever to have recourse to thee, O Mother of Perpetual Help!

5 Hail Marys, and prayer as above.

Indulgence of 500 days. (No. 392)

PRAYER TO OUR DEAR MOTHER OF PERPETUAL HELP.

Virgin, dearest Mother mine,
Let me be forever thine;
Thine throughout my earthly life,
Thine in sorrow, fear, and strife;
Thine, when dark'ning clouds will lower,
Thine,—thine own, through thy great power.
Virgin sweet, O Mother mine,
Let me be forever Thine.
Mother—I trust and confide in thee!
Mother—I send up my sighs to thee!
Mother—assist thy poor child so weak!
Mother—protection and strength I seek!
O Mother—come, teach me how to pray!
O Mother—come, help in my combat each day!
O Mother—come, teach me to suffer like thee!
O Mother—yes, come, be forever with me!
Yes, thou canst help me, most Powerful one!
Thou shalt sustain me, most Merciful one!
Thou must assist me, most Faithful one!
O yes, thou wilt aid me, most Loving one!
Mother of grace, the joy of our nation!
Refuge of sinners, the gate of salvation!
Hope of the exile, God's work of perfection!

Comfort in sorrow, our mighty protection!
Who ever implored thee in vain, Mother mild,
When hast thou forgotten the pray'rs of thy child?
I call, without ceasing, in sadness or fear:
"Sweet Mary will aid me, Mother so dear!"
I call in all suff'ring, and with my last breath:
"O Mary, assist me, in life and in death!"
This is my fond hope, and at last I shall say:
"My Mother will meet me in Heaven today!"

The Archconfraternity of Our Lady of Perpetual Help and St. Alphonsus is established at this Church.

1.—**Advantages.** The special protection of Our Blessed Lady in life and in death. Many plenary and partial indulgences.

2.—**Obligations.** None that bind under sin. The following practices are recommended; to wear a medal of Our Lady of Perpetual Help; to have her picture in one's room; on Wednesdays if possible to visit the picture in our church, which is an exact copy of the miraculous image in Rome; in all spiritual and temporal necessities to invoke the help of Our Blessed Lady.

3.—**Reception.** Nothing else is required than to have one's name enrolled in the register. Non-residents may be enrolled provided they express their intention through a friend or apply by letter.

Novena Booklet, Medal and Picture can be had for a small fee.

The Thirty Days' Prayer

TO THE BLESSED VIRGIN MARY IN HONOR OF THE SACRED PASSION OF OUR LORD JESUS CHRIST.

Ever glorious and blessed Mary, Queen of Virgins, Mother of Mercy, hope and comfort of dejected and desolate souls, through that sword of sorrow which pierced thy tender heart whilst thine only Son, Jesus Christ, our Lord, suffered death and ignominy on the Cross; through that filial tenderness and pure love He had for thee, grieving in thy grief, whilst from His Cross He recommended thee to the care and protection of His beloved disciple, St. John, take pity, I beseech thee, on my poverty and necessities; have compassion on my anxieties and cares; assist and comfort me in all my infirmities and miseries, of what kind soever. Thou art the Mother of Mercies, the sweet comforter and refuge of the needy and the orphan, of the desolate and the afflicted. Cast, therefore, an eye of pity on a miserable forlorn child of Eve, and hear my prayer; for since, in just punishment of my sins, I find myself encompassed by a multitude of evils, and oppressed with much anguish of spirit, whither can I fly for more secure shelter, O amiable Mother of my Lord and Saviour, Jesus Christ, than under the wings of thy maternal protection? Attend, therefore, I beseech thee, with an ear of pity and compassion, to my humble and earnest request. I ask it, through the bowels of mercy of thy dear Son; through that love and condescension wherewith He embraced our nature, when, in compliance with the Divine will, thou gavest thy consent, and Whom, after the expiration of nine months, thou didst bring forth from the chaste enclosure of thy womb, to visit this world, and bless it with His presence. I ask it, through that anguish of mind wherewith thy beloved Son, our dear Saviour, was overwhelmed on Mount Olivet, when He besought His eternal Father to remove from Him, if possible, the bitter chalice of His future passion. I ask it, through the threefold repetition of His prayers in the garden, whence afterwards, with dolorous steps and mournful tears, thou didst accompany Him to the doleful theatre of His death and sufferings. I ask it, through the welts and bruises of His virginal Flesh, occasioned by the cords and whips wherewith He was bound and scourged when stripped of His seamless garment, for which His executioners afterwards cast lots. I ask it, through the scoffs and ignominies by which He was insulted; the false accusations and unjust sentence by which He was condemned to death, and which He bore with heavenly patience. I ask it, through His bitter tears and bloody sweat, His silence and resignation, His sadness and grief of heart. I ask it, through the blood which trickled from His royal and sacred head when struck with the sceptre of a reed, and pierced with His crown of thorns. I ask it, through the excruciating torments He suffered, when His hands and feet were fastened with gross nails to the tree of the Cross. I ask it, through His vehement thirst and bitter potion of vinegar and gall. I ask it, through His dereliction on the Cross, when He exclaimed: "My God! My God! why hast Thou forsaken Me?" I ask it, through His mercy extended to the good thief, and through His recommending His precious soul and spirit into the hands of His eternal Father before He expired, saying: "All is consummated." I ask it through the blood mixed with water, which issued from His sacred Side the efficacy of thy powerful intercession, according to the tenderness of thy maternal affection, and His filial loving Heart, Who mercifully granteth the requests, and complieth with the desires of those that love and fear Him. Wherefore, O most Blessed Virgin, besides the object of my present petition, and whatever else I may stand in need of, obtain for me also of thy dear Son, our Lord and our God, a lively faith, firm hope, perfect charity, true contrition of heart, unfeigned tears of compunction, sincere confession, condign satisfaction, abstinence from sin, love of God and my neighbor, contempt of the world, patience to suffer affronts and ignominies, nay, even, if necessary, an opprobrius death itself, for love of thy Son, our Saviour, Jesus Christ. Obtain likewise for me, O sacred Mother of God, perseverance in good works, performance of good resolutions, mortification of self-will, a pious conversation through life, and at my last moments, strong and sincere repentance, accompanied by such a lively and attentive presence of mind as may enable me to receive the last Sacraments of the Church worthily, and die in thy friendship and favor. Lastly, obtain, I beseech thee, for the souls of my parents, brethren, relatives, and benefactors, both living and dead, life everlasting. Amen.

Prayer to St. Joachim.

O great and glorious patriarch St. Joachim, how I rejoice in the thought that thou wast selected from among all the saints to cooperate in the divine mysteries, and to enrich the world with the great Mother of God, Mary most holy! By this special privilege thou didst become most powerful with the Mother and with the Son, so that there is no grace, however great, which thou canst not obtain. Animated with such confidence, I have recourse to thy powerful protection, and recommend to thee all my needs, and those of my family, both spiritual and temporal, but particularly the special grace which I desire and expect from thy fatherly intercession. And as thou wert a perfect model of the interior life, obtain for me the grace of recollection and detachment from the fleeting goods of this earth, with a lively and persevering love for Jesus and Mary. Obtain for me, also, sincere devotion and obedience to Holy Church, and to the Sovereign Pontiff governing it, that I may live and die in faith, hope, and perfect charity, invoking the holy names of Jesus and Mary, and thus be saved. Amen.

*Indulgence of 300 days, once a day. (No. 453)

Prayer to Good St. Anne.

With a heart full of sincere, filial

veneration, I prostrate myself before thee, O blessed St. Anne! Thou art that beloved and privileged creature who, because of thy extraordinary virtue and sanctity, didst deserve of God the supreme grace of giving life to the treasury of grace, the blessed among women, the Mother of the Incarnate Lord, the Blessed Virgin Mary.

Ah! in consideration of such exalted favors, deign, O most tender saint, to receive me among the number of thy devoted servants, for such I protest myself to be, and wish to remain for the rest of my life. Surround me with thy efficacious patronage, and obtain for me, from God, the imitation of those virtues with which thou wert so profusely adorned.

Obtain for me a knowledge of my sins, and sorrow for them; an ardent love for Jesus and Mary; a faithful and constant observance of the duties of my state of life. Save me from all dangers in life, and assist me at the hour of my death, that I may safely reach Paradise, there to praise with thee, most happy mother, the Word of God made man in the womb of thy most pure daughter, the Blessed Virgin Mary. Amen.

*Indulgence of 300 days, once a day. (No. 456)

Prayer to St. Joseph.
(To be said especially after the Rosary.)

To thee, O blessed Joseph, we have recourse in our affliction, and, having implored the help of thy thrice holy Spouse, we now, with hearts filled with confidence, earnestly beg thee also to take us under thy protection. By that charity, wherewith thou wert united to the Immaculate Virgin, Mother of God, and by that fatherly love, with which thou didst cherish the Child Jesus, we beseech thee and we humbly pray that thou wilt look down with gracious eyes upon that inheritance which Jesus Christ purchased by His Blood, and wilt succor us in our need by thy power and strength.

Defend, O most watchful guardian of the Holy Family, the chosen offspring of Jesus Christ. Keep from us, O most loving Father, all blight of error and corruption. Aid us from on high, most valiant defender, in this conflict with the powers of darkness, and even as of old, thou didst rescue the Child Jesus from the peril of His life, so now defend God's Holy Church from the snares of the enemy and from all adversity. Shield us ever under thy patronage, that, imitating thy example and strengthened by thy help, we may live a holy life, die a happy death, and attain everlasting bliss in Heaven. Amen.

*Indulgence of three years. In October after reciting the Rosary, an indulgence of seven years. (No. 438)

Invocation of St. Joseph.

Help us, Joseph, in our earthly strife,
E'er to lead a pure and blameless life.

*Indulgence of 300 days. (No. 421)

Prayer to the Angel Guardian.

Angel of God, my Guardian dear,
To whom His love commits me here,
Ever this day be at my side
To light and guard, to rule and guide.
　Amen.

*Three hundred days' indulgence, also plenary indulgence at the hour of death. (No. 415)

Prayer to St. Anthony of Padua.

If then you ask for miracles,
　Death, error, all calamities,
The leprosy and demons fly,
　And health succeeds infirmities.

The sea obeys, and fetters break,
　And lifeless limbs thou dost restore;
Whilst treasures lost are found again,
　When young and old thine aid implore.

All dangers vanish at thy prayer,
 And direst need doth quickly flee;
Let those who know, thy power proclaim,
 Let Paduans say: These are of thee.

The sea obeys, and fetters break,
 And lifeless limbs thou dost restore;
Whilst treasures lost are found again,
 When young and old thine aid implore.

To the Father, Son, may glory be
 And Holy Ghost eternally.

The sea obeys, etc.

V. Pray for us, blessed Anthony.

R. That we may be made worthy of the promises of Christ.

Let us pray.

O God! may the votive commemoration of blessed Anthony, Thy confessor, be a source of joy to Thy Church, that she may always be fortified with spiritual assistance, and deserve to enjoy eternal rewards. Through Christ, our Lord. Amen.

*300 days' indulgence once a day. (No. 491)

Litany

IN HONOR OF ST. ALPHONSUS MARIA DE LIGUORI.

(Taken from the Manual C. SS. R.)

Bishop, Doctor of the Church, and Founder of the Order of Redemptorists. Born 1696; died 1787; canonized 1839; feast, Aug. 2nd.

Lord, have mercy on us.
Christ, have mercy on us.
Lord, have mercy on us.
Christ, hear us.
Christ, graciously hear us.
God the Father of Heaven, *Have mercy on us.*
God the Son, Redeemer of the world, *Have mercy on us.*
God the Holy Ghost, *Have mercy on us.*
Holy Trinity, one God, *Have mercy on us.*

Holy Mary, Virgin Immaculate,
St. Alphonsus, model of piety from tenderest youth,
St. Alphonsus, scourge of heresies,
St. Alphonsus, defender of the Catholic faith,
St. Alphonsus, always occupied in evangelizing the poor,
St. Alphonsus, tender comforter of the afflicted,
St. Alphonsus, instructed in the Divine art of converting sinners,
St. Alphonsus, enlightened guide in the path of perfection,

} *Pray for us*

LITANY OF ST. ALPHONSUS

St. Alphonsus, who became all things to all men, to gain all for Jesus Christ,
St. Alphonsus, new ornament of the Religious state,
St. Alphonsus, bold champion of ecclesiastical discipline,
St. Alphonsus, model of submission and devotion to the Sovereign Pontiff,
St. Alphonsus, who didst watch unceasingly over the flock committed to thee,
St. Alphonsus, full of solicitude for the common good of the Church,
St. Alphonsus, glory of the Priesthood and of the Episcopate,
St. Alphonsus, shining mirror of all virtues,
St. Alphonsus, full of tenderest love for the infant Jesus,
St. Alphonsus, inflamed with divine love whilst offering the Holy Sacrifice of the Mass,
St. Alphonsus, fervent adorer of Jesus Christ in the Holy Eucharist,
St. Alphonsus, penetrated with lively compassion while meditating on the sufferings of our Divine Saviour,
St. Alphonsus, specially devoted to the Blessed Virgin Mary,
St. Alphonsus, favored by apparitions of the Mother of God,
St. Alphonsus, leading an angelic life,
St. Alphonsus, a true Patriarch in thy paternal solicitude for the people of God,
St. Alphonsus, endowed with the gift of prophecy and miracles,
St. Alphonsus, an Apostle by the extent and fruit of thy labors,
St. Alphonsus, a Martyr by thy austerities,
St. Alphonsus, a Confessor by thy writings full of the Spirit of God,

Pray for us

St. Alphonsus, a Virgin by thy purity of soul and body,
St. Alphonsus, a model of Missionaries,
St. Alphonsus, founder of the Order of the Most Holy Redeemer,
St. Alphonsus, our tender father and powerful protector,

Pray for us

Lamb of God, Who takest away the sins of the world, *Spare us, O Lord.*
Lamb of God, Who takest away the sins of the world, *Graciously hear us, O Lord.*
Lamb of God, Who takest away the sins of the world, *Have mercy on us.*

Christ, hear us. *Christ graciously hear us.*
Pray for us, St. Alphonsus,
That we may be made worthy of the promises of Christ.

Let us pray.

(Prayer of the Church.)

O God, Who by the Blessed Alphonsus Maria, Thy Confessor and Bishop, inflamed with zeal for souls, has enriched Thy Church with a new progeny: we beseech Thee, that taught by his saving counsels, and strengthened by his example, we may happily come to Thee. Through Christ, our Lord. Amen.

Prayers

IN HONOR OF SAINT CLEMENT MARIA HOFBAUER,

Priest of the Congregation of the Most Holy Redeemer. Born 1751; died 1820; beatified 1888; canonized May 20, 1909; feast, March 15th.

O Saint Clement, *most faithful disciple of Jesus,* our Redeemer, from thy tenderest infancy thou didst regard only holy Catholic Faith as thy only treasure, and wast solicitous to strengthen it in the hearts of the faithful with wonderful zeal, and to make it known among men. Obtain for us the grace to imitate thy example and to learn to esteem the precious gift of the true Faith above every other gift. Teach us to conform our actions to its holy maxims, so that, placing in the practice of Faith all our glory, we may exultingly repeat thy own words:

"We confess, we are sinners, and

devoid of every virtue, but we glory in the fact that we are children of Holy Catholic Church".

Our Father, Hail Mary, Glory be, etc.

II.

O Saint Clement, *most constant disciple of Jesus,* our Redeemer, mistrusting thyself and placing no reliance in the aid and counsels of men, thou didst repose all thy confidence in God alone. Strengthened by this firm hope, thou didst despise all the goods, pleasures and honors of the world, fixing thy eyes on Heaven, where joys are eternal and goods are imperishable. Obtain for us the grace to follow thy example by detaching ourselves from the things of this earth. Teach us to direct all our affections towards Heaven, confidently hoping from God, by means of holy prayer, the assistance necessary to effect this; mindful of the grand maxim which thou didst repeat from thy earliest years:

"We must devote to prayer the time that remains after the discharge of the duties of our state of life."

Our Father, Hail Mary, Glory be, etc.

III.

O Saint Clement, *most loving disciple of Jesus,* our Redeemer, animated by the most ardent charity, thou didst live for God alone, and didst make thyself all to all to gain all for Jesus Christ. Persecutions and dangers, temptations and sufferings, were not able to diminish thy charity. Obtain for us, we implore thee, at least a spark of thy most burning love for God and our neighbor. Aid us by thy prayers *to be so united in harmony and charity that we may always love our most loving Redeemer, Jesus Christ and His Immaculate Mother, follow*

Him steadfastly until death, and finally praise and bless Him for all eternity.

Our Father, Hail Mary, Glory be, etc.

V. Pray for us, O Saint Clement.

R. That we may be made worthy of the promises of Christ.

Let us pray.

(Prayer of the Church.)

O God, Who didst adorn the Blessed Clement with wonderful strength of faith and with the virtue of constancy, through his merits and example, make us, we beseech Thee, so steadfast in faith and burning with charity, that we may obtain the eternal rewards. Through Christ, our Lord. Amen.

Litany

In Honor of St. Gerard Majella, Lay-Brother of the Congregation of the Most Holy Redeemer.

Born 1726; died 1755; beatified 1893; canonized Dec. 11th, 1904; feast, Oct. 16th.

Lord, have mercy on us.
Christ, have mercy on us.
Lord have mercy on us.
Christ, hear us.
Christ graciously hear us.
God the Father of Heaven, *Have mercy on us.*
God the Son, Redeemer of the world, *Have mercy on us.*
God the Holy Ghost, *Have mercy on us.*
Holy Trinity, one God, *Have mercy on us.*

Holy Mary, Mother of Perpetual Help,
St. Joseph, foster-father of Christ,
St. Alphonsus, founder of the Congregation of the Most Holy Redeemer,
St. Gerard, enriched with extraordinary graces from early youth,
St. Gerard, perfect model of a faithful servant,
St. Gerard, bright pattern of the working classes,
St. Gerard, great lover of prayer and work,
St. Gerard, seraph of love towards the Blessed Sacrament,
St. Gerard, living image of the crucified Saviour,
St. Gerard, zealous client of the Immaculate Virgin Mary,
St. Gerard, bright mirror of innocence and penance,
St. Gerard, admirable model of heroic obedience,

Pray for us

LITANY OF ST. GERARD MAJELLA

St. Gerard, silent victim of ignominious calumny,
St. Gerard, great before God by thy deep humility,
St. Gerard, truly wise by thy childlike simplicity,
St. Gerard, supernaturally enlightened in divine mysteries,
St. Gerard, solely desirous of pleasing God,
St. Gerard, zealous promoter of the conversion of sinners,
St. Gerard, wise counsellor in the choice of vocation,
St. Gerard, enlightened guide in the direction of souls,
St. Gerard, loving friend of the poor and afflicted,
St. Gerard, safe refuge in sickness and sorrow,
St. Gerard, wonderful protector of unbaptized children,
St. Gerard, compassionate intercessor in every necessity,
St. Gerard, honor and glory of the Redemptorist Order,

} *Pray for us*

Lamb of God, Who takest away the sins of the world, *Spare us, O Lord!*
Lamb of God, Who takest away the sins of the world, *Graciously hear us, O Lord!*
Lamb of God, Who takest away the sins of the world, *Have mercy on us!*
Pray for us St. Gerard.
That we may be made worthy of the promises of Christ.

Let us pray.

O God, Who wast pleased to draw to Thyself the Blessed Gerard from his youth, and to render him conformable to the image of Thy crucified Son, grant, we beseech Thee, that following his example we may be transformed into the selfsame image, Through the same Christ, our Lord. Amen.

Short Indulgenced Prayers

Applicable to the Holy Souls.

"My Lord God, even now resignedly and willingly I accept at Thy hand with all its anxieties, pains and sufferings, whatever kind of death it shall please Thee to be mine."

Indulgence of seven years, plenary at hour of death. (No. 591)

1. My loving Jesus, I, N. N., give Thee my heart, and I consecrate myself wholly to Thee out of the grateful love I bear Thee, and as a reparation for all my unfaithfulness; and with Thy aid, I purpose never to sin again.

*300 days' indulgence to those who recite this prayer before an image of the Sacred Heart of Jesus. (No. 228)

SHORT IND. PRAYERS 275

2. Jesus, meek and humble of Heart, make my heart like unto Thine.

*500 days' indulgence. (No. 196)

3. May the Sacred Heart of Jesus be loved everywhere.

300 days' indulgence. (No. 192)

4. May the Heart of Jesus in the Most Blessed Sacrament, be praised, adored, and loved with grateful affection, at every moment, in all the tabernacles of the world, even to the end of time.

300 days' indulgence. (No. 246)

5. Jesus, my God. I love Thee above all things.

300 days' indulgence. (No. 57)

6. My Jesus, mercy.

*300 days' indulgence. (No. 55)

* 7. Eternal Father! I offer Thee the precious Blood of Jesus in satisfaction for my sins, and for the wants of the Holy Church.

*500 days' indulgence. (No. 188)

8. Sweet Heart of Jesus, I implore that I may ever love Thee more and more.

*300 days' indulgence. (No. 193)

9. Sweet Heart of Mary, be my salvation.

*300 days' indulgence. (No. 352)

10. Blessed be the holy and Immaculate Conception of the Most Blessed Virgin Mary, Mother of God.

*300 days' indulgence. (No. 324)

11. O Mary, who didst come into this world free from stain, obtain of God for me that I may leave it without sin.

300 days' indulgence. (No. 323)

12. Mother of Perpetual Help, pray for us.

300 days' indulgence. (No. 391)

13. Jesus, Mary, and Joseph, I give you my heart and my soul. Jesus Mary, and Joseph assist me in my

last agony. Jesus, Mary and Joseph, may I breathe forth my soul in peace with you.

*Seven years' for each invocation. (No. 589)

14. May the most just, most high, and most amiable will of God be done in all things, be praised and magnified forever.

*500 days' indulgence. (No. 4)

15. O most compassionate Jesus! Thou alone art our salvation, our life, and our resurrection. We implore Thee, therefore, do not forsake us in our needs and afflictions, but by the agony of Thy most Sacred Heart, and by the sorrows of Thy immaculate Mother, succor Thy servants, whom Thou hast redeemed by Thy most precious Blood.

One hundred days' indulgence, once a day.

16. In the name of the Father, and of the Son, and of the Holy Ghost.

*100 days' indulgence every time for making the sign of the cross, using the above words. Three hundred days if made with holy water. (No. 631)

17. O Sacrament most holy! O Sacrament Divine! All praise and all thanksgiving be every moment Thine.

*300 days' indulgence. (No. 110)

18. Bid me bear, O Mother blessed!
On my heart the wounds impressed
Suffered by the Crucified.

*500 days' indulgence. (No. 341)

19. Immaculate Queen of Peace, pray for us.

300 days' indulgence. (No. 395)

20. Eternal rest grant unto them, O Lord: and let perpetual light shine upon them. May they rest in peace. Amen.

300 days' indulgence each time, for the souls in Purgatory only. (No. 536)

THE TEN COMMANDMENTS OF GOD.

1. I am the Lord thy God. Thou shalt not have strange gods before Me.

2. Thou shalt not take the name of the Lord thy God in vain.

3. Remember thou keep holy the Sabbath day.

4. Honor thy father and thy mother.

5. Thou shalt not kill.

6. Thou shalt not commit adultery.

7. Thou shalt not steal.

8. Thou shalt not bear false witness against thy neighbor.

9. Thou shalt not covet thy neighbor's wife.

10. Thou shalt not covet thy neighbor's goods.

THE CHIEF COMMANDMENTS OF THE CHURCH.

1. To hear Mass on Sundays and Holydays of obligation.

2. To fast and abstain on the days appointed.

3. To confess at least once a year.

4. To receive the Holy Eucharist during the Easter time.

5. To contribute to the support of our pastors.

6. Not to marry persons who are not Catholics, or who are related to us within the third degree of consanguinity or the second degree of affinity, nor privately without witnesses, nor to solemnize marriage at forbidden times.

FESTIVALS OF OBLIGATION.

In addition to the Sundays, the following are Holydays of obligation in every diocese of the United States:

Immaculate Conception, Dec. 8.
Nativity of our Lord, Dec. 25.
Circumcision, Jan. 1.
Assumption, Aug. 15.
Ascension, forty days after Easter.
All Saints, Nov. 1.

HEROIC ACT OF LOVE,

OR OFFERING OF ALL THE SATISFACTORY WORKS FOR THE RELIEF OF THE SUFFERING SOULS IN PURGATORY.

I, N. N., renounce in favor of the suffering souls in Purgatory the satisfactory portion of all the good works which, with the assistance of divine grace, I from this day shall perform, as also all the prayers and satisfactory works which may, after my death, be applied to my benefit, and I place them all in the hands of the Most Blessed Virgin, that this Mother of Mercy may dispose of them according to her pleasure.

I. The Indult of a Privileged Altar, personally, every day in the year to all priests who shall have made this offering.

II. A Plenary Indulgence daily, applicable only to the departed, to all the faithful, who shall have made this offering, whenever they go to Holy Communion, provided they visit a church or public oratory, and pray there for some time for the intention of his Holiness.

III. A Plenary Indulgence, every Monday, to all who hear Mass in aid of the souls in Purgatory, provided they fulfill the other conditions mentioned above. (No. 547.)

INDEX

	Page
Preface	5
Indulgenced Prayers for the Suffering Souls	9
First Day, Prayers for the Holy Souls	10
Second Day, Anniversary of "All Souls"	13
Third Day, The Doctrine of Purgatory	15
Fourth Day, Expiation for Venial Sins and Imperfections	17
Fifth Day, The Suffering of Purgatory	20
Sixth Day, The Pain of Loss	22
Seventh Day, Pain of Sorrow for Sin	24
Eighth Day, Pain of Helplessness and Desolation	27
Ninth Day, the Pain of Fire in Purgatory	29
Tenth Day, The Duration of Purgatory	32
Eleventh Day, Our Duty to Relieve the Souls in Purgatory	34
Twelfth Day, Grand Display is of no Value to the Holy Souls	37
Thirteenth Day, The Special Duty of Every One to Aid the Faithful Departed	39
Fourteenth Day, The Special Duty of Children Towards their Deceased Parents	41
Fifteenth Day, The State of Grace Necessary to Assist the Souls in Purgatory	43
Sixteenth Day, The Efficacy of Prayer for the Suffering Souls	45
Seventeenth Day, The Manner in which the Church bestows Indulgences upon the Souls in Purgatory	47
Eighteenth Day, The Efficacy of Holy Mass for the Departed	50
Nineteenth Day, Holy Communion of Great Benefit to the Departed	53
Twentieth Day, Love of the Blessed Virgin towards the Souls in Purgatory	55

INDEX

	Page
Twenty-first Day, Efficacy of the Rosary for the Suffering Souls	58
Twenty-second Day, Alms-giving Affords Great Relief to the Departed	60
Twenty-third Day, Works of Penance for the Holy Souls	63
Twenty-fourth Day, Value of Good Works for the Suffering Souls	65
Twenty-fifth Day, Gratitude of the Holy Souls	67
Twenty-sixth Day, By Delivering the Souls from Purgatory we promote the honor of God	70
Twenty-seventh Day, The Lord Rewards Charity towards the Holy Souls	72
Twenty-eighth Day, They have great reason to fear, who show no mercy towards the Souls departed	74
Twenty-ninth Day, Perseverance in Prayer for the Departed	77
Thirtieth Day, The Heroic Act of Charity for the Souls in Purgatory	79
Thirty-first Day, By a good intention to make even our most trivial actions and sufferings meritorious, and offer them for the deliverance of the Holy Souls	83
A Short meditation for every Day	86
Morning Prayer by St. Alphonsus	87
The Angelus	88
To-Day	90
Good intention "Solely God's Glory"	91
Prayers before and after meals	93
Evening devotions, Faith, Hope and Charity, etc. The "Memorare" of S. Bernard	96
Devotions for Confession	99
"No more Sin"	103
Acts before Holy Communion	104
Acts after Holy Communion	109

INDEX

	Page
Soul of Christ, sanctify me	113
The Indulgenced Prayer: "Look down upon me," etc.	114
Prayer for the Faithful Departed	115
"All for Jesus"	116
Mass in honor of the Passion	118
Mass for the Dead	133
Indulgenced Prayers after Mass	157
Visit to the Blessed Sacrament, by St. Alphonsus	159
Divine Praises	162
Daily Offering to the S. Heart	163
Prayer for the Dying	164
Litany of the S. Heart	165
Consecration to the S. Heart	168
Visit to the Blessed Virgin	170
The Magnificat of the Blessed Virgin	172
Litany of the Blessed Virgin	173
The Mysteries of the Holy Rosary	177
Rosary of the Blessed Virgin, blessed by The Crosier Fathers	179
Beads of the Seven Dolors	181
Lay Baptism	184
The Sign of the Cross	185
The Doxology	185
The Lord's Prayer	185
The Angelical Salutation	186
The Apostles' Creed	186
Six Truths we must Know and Believe	187
Prayer to Christ the King	188
Prayer to St. Alphonsus	189
Indulgences for the Way of the Cross	190
"Stations of the Cross," by St. Alphonsus	192
Stabat Mater (At the Cross her station keeping)	207
Protestation for a Happy Death, by St. Alphonsus	211
Prayer for a good Death	215
Eternity	220
Prayer of a soul in Desolation	223
Explanation of a Novena	223

INDEX

	Page
Novena for the Holy Souls in Purgatory	225
Prayer to our Suffering Savior for Souls in Purgatory	227
De Profundis (Out of the Depths)	239
Act of Consecration to the Holy Family	240
Prayer to be said every day before a Picture of the Holy Family	242
Three Days' Prayer in honor of Our Lady of Perpetual Help	243
Triduo	244
Prayer to our dear Mother of Perpetual Help	249
The Thirty Days' prayer to the Blessed Virgin in honor of the Passion of our Lord	251
Prayer to St. Joachim	258
Prayer to good St. Anne	259
Prayer to St. Joseph especially after the Rosary	261
Invocation of St. Joseph	263
Prayer to the Angel Guardian	263
Prayer to St. Anthony of Padua	263
Litany in honor of St. Alphonsus	265
Three Prayers to Saint Clement Maria Hofbauer C.SS.R.	268
Litany in Honor of Saint Gerard Majella, C.SS.R.	272
Short Indulgenced Prayers, applicable to the Souls in Purgatory	274
The Ten Commandments of God	278
The Chief Commandment of the Church	279
Heroic Act	280
Festivals of Obligation	280

The following is a special excerpt from:
The Manual of the Holy Catholic Church
Copyright 1906

"The Soul in Perfect Charity with God"

Jacobus Eduardus

Archiepiscopus Chicagiensis.

Imprimatur,
† James Edward,
Archbishop of Chicago.

Chicago Ill.
Aug 24th 1906,

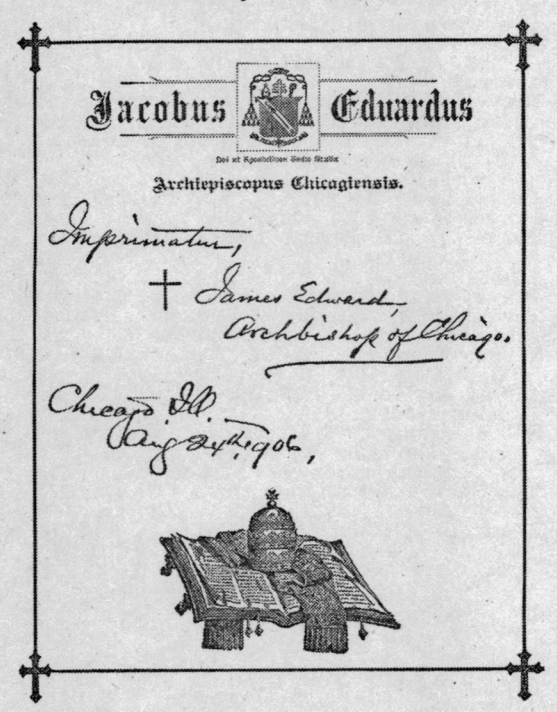

The Soul in Perfect Charity with God

INSTRUCTIONS ON PURGATORY

Q. What does our Holy Faith teach us concerning Purgatory?

A. That, after this life, there is a middle state of suffering, to which the souls of those are condemned for a time, who though dying in the state of grace, and in friendship with God, yet have not fully satisfied the Divine Justice for the debt of temporal punishment due for their smaller sins; or for their more grievous sins, whose guilt has been pardoned in the Sacrament of Penance; or who die under the guilt of smaller sins or imperfections.

Q. Upon what grounds is this doctrine of Purgatory founded?

A. Upon these following: *First*, As the justice of God absolutely demands from sinners a reparation of the injury done to him by sin, by means of temporal punishments to be undergone by them after the guilt of their mortal sins, and the eternal punishment has been remitted and forgiven them; and, as this debt of temporal punishment is increased by the venial sins they commit, which also being offensive to God, must be punished by the Divine Justice; for "God will render to every man according to his works," and of every idle word we speak, an account will be demanded; hence it necessarily follows, that there must be a state of temporal punishment after death, where all those must go, who, dying in the state of grace, have not paid this debt before they die, and where they must remain in suffering till such time as they have fully paid it. This place cannot be Heaven; for in Heaven there can be no suffering. It cannot be Hell; for out of Hell there can be no redemption, and those who die in the state of grace, cannot be condemned for ever; therefore it must be a middle place distinct from both.

On these grounds our Savior describes the nature of this state as follows, making use of it as a powerful motive to engage us to live a truly penitential life here, that we may clear that debt before we die: "Be at agreement with thy adversary quickly," says he, "whilst thou art in the way with him, least perhaps the adversary deliver thee to the judge, and the judge deliver thee to the officer, and thou be cast into prison; amen, I say to thee, thou shalt not go out from thence till thou pay the last farthing," Matth. v. 25. Here we see the doctrine of the Purgatory described to us in the plainest terms.

This present life is everywhere represented in the holy scriptures as *a way* in which we are traveling towards Eternity. Our *adversary* is the Divine Justice to whom we owe the debt of temporal punishment. God himself is the *judge*. If therefore, we do not satisfy our adversary during this life, while we are in the way, when we come to die, and be presented before the Judge, we shall be condemned to purgatory, where we must remain, till by our sufferings we have fully satisfied the Divine Justice for the debt we owe, even to the last farthing.

VENIAL SINS GREATLY DEFILE AND OBSCURE THE PURITY OF THE SOUL.

Second, We have seen that though venial sins do not banish the grace of God from the soul, nor break our friendship with God, nor condemn us to eternal punishments, yet they greatly defile and obscure the purity of the soul, and render it less agreeable in the eyes of God; now, the word of God assures us, that "there shall not enter into Heaven any thing defiled," Rev. xxi. 27; and that none "but the clean of heart shall see God," Matth. v. 8. When, therefore, a soul leaves this world in perfect charity with God, clean and undefiled by even the smallest stains of sin, doubtless that soul will immediately be admitted into the presence and enjoyment of God. If, on the contrary, the soul leaves this world in disgrace with God, and dead to him by the guilt of mortal sin, that soul will undoubtedly be condemned to the eternal torments of hell. But when a soul leaves this world in the friendship of God, but sullied with the stains of smaller venial sins, it is plain such a soul cannot in that state go to heaven, where "nothing defiled can enter;" neither can it be condemned to hell, because it is in friendship with God, and a living member of Jesus Christ; therefore there must be some middle state, where such a soul is confined for a time, till by suffering it be cleansed and purged from all these defilements of venial sins, and rendered fit to be admitted to the presence and enjoyment of God.

In this view, our blessed Savior says, "he that shall speak against the Holy Ghost, it shall not be forgiven him, neither in this world, nor in the world to come," Matth. xii. 32. In which words he plainly insinuates, that some sins shall be forgiven in the world to come, otherwise it would be superfluous and trifling to say of the sin of the Holy Ghost in particular, that it shall never be forgiven neither in this world nor in the next. To the same purpose the prophet Isaiah says, "The voice of the Lord of hosts was revealed in my ears, surely this iniquity shall not be forgiven till ye die, saith the Lord God of hosts," Is. xxii. 14; which plainly implies that, after death, it should be forgiven them.

This truth necessarily establishes a middle state, where some sins shall be forgiven; this place cannot be heaven, for no sin can enter there to be forgiven; it cannot be hell, for in hell there is no forgiveness; therefore, it must be a middle place, distinct from both. Neither can these sins which are forgiven in the next life be mortal sins; for a soul that dies in mortal sin is immediately condemned to hell, like the rich glutton in the gospel: therefore, they are only venial sins which are purged from the soul in purgatory, as here explained.

Third, From what has been said, it appears, 1. That the souls who go to Purgatory are only such as die in the state of grace, united to Jesus Christ. 2. That it is their imperfect works for which they are condemned to that place of suffering, and which must all be there consumed, and their stains purged away from them, before they can go to heaven. 3. That, however, they shall at last be saved, and received into eternal bliss, to wit, when they have paid the utmost farthing, and when all their imperfections are purged away. This is the precise doctrine of the Church concerning purgatory. This doctrine is laid down by St. Paul in the plainest terms as follows: "For other foundation no man can lay, but that which is laid; which is Christ Jesus;" that is, none can be saved but such as are united to Jesus Christ by faith, that worketh by charity: "Now, if any man build upon this foundation, gold, silver, precious stones, wood, hay, stubble, every man's work shall be manifest; for the day of the Lord shall declare it, because it shall be revealed by fire, and the fire shall try every man's works, of what sort it is." The building upon this foundation, as here explained, signifies the works that a man performs while united to Jesus Christ; such works as are good and perfect, are compared to gold, silver, and precious stones; such as are imperfect and venially sinful, are compared to wood, hay, stubble.

At the day of the Lord, at the particular judgment after death, all these works shall be tried and examined by him, for then, *the fire of*

God's judgment shall "try every man's works of what sort it is." If any man's works abide which he hath built thereupon, he shall receive a reward, and be immediately admitted into the joy of his Lord; "if any man's works burn, he shall suffer loss," these works being found of no value, he must suffer for them; yet, having built upon the right foundation, by living and dying in the state of grace, and united to Jesus Christ, though with much imperfection, "he himself shall be saved, yet so as by fire," being liable to this punishment on account of his many imperfections, 1 Cor. iii. 11. On this text of scripture, St. Ambrose says as follows: "Whereas St. Paul saith *yet so as by fire,* he showeth indeed, that he shall be saved, but yet shall suffer the punishment of fire; that being purged by fire, he may be saved, and not tormented forever," Ser. 20., in Psal. 118.

THE PRACTICE OF PRAYING FOR THE SOULS OF THE DEAD MORE ANCIENT THAN CHRISTIANITY.

Fourth, The belief of a Purgatory, and the practice of praying for the souls detained there, is far from being a novelty, introduced in latter ages, as the enemies of the Catholic Church pretend.

It is much more ancient than Christianity itself; and we have a most decisive proof of it from scripture, among the people of God under the old law, in the time of Judas Machabeus, about two hundred years before Christ. For, upon a great victory gained by that valiant general over the enemies of their religion, after the battle, in which many of his people had been slain, "Judas, making a gathering, he sent twelve thousand drachms of silver to Jerusalem for a sacrifice to be offered for the sins of the dead, thinking well and religiously concerning the resurrection—and because he considered that they who had fallen asleep, with godliness, had great grace laid up for them.

A HOLY AND WHOLESOME THOUGHT TO PRAY FOR THE DEAD.

"It is, therefore, a holy and wholesome thought to pray for the dead, that they may be loosed from sins," 2 Macca. xii. 46. In this passage of holy writ, we have the following particulars established: *First,* That the whole people of God, long before Christ, did hold it holy and laudable to pray for the dead.

Second, That they believed this to be a means

of benefiting the souls departed, by freeing them from their sins.

Third, That the word of God declares this to be *holy* and *wholesome.* If therefore the souls of the faithful departed are benefited by the prayers of those upon earth, this establishes a Purgatory beyond all contradiction, since those in Heaven are in need of no help, and those in Hell can receive none. We do not find that our Savior ever reprehended the Jews for this practice, though upon all occasions, he censured the Pharisees for the observances they had introduced, some of which were even of much less consequence than this.

Q. Are the sufferings of the souls in Purgatory very severe?

A. They are certainly most dreadful; much more so than any thing we can conceive in this world. *First,* Because the scripture says they shall "be saved, yet so as by fire," I Cor. iii.

Second, Because they are wholly in the hands of the Divine Justice, and the scripture says, "It is a fearful thing to fall into the hands of the living God," Heb. x. 31. And, indeed, even in this life, where his justice is always mixed with mercy, how dreadful are his punishments upon sinners! Witness the many examples in scripture, even for sins, which to us would seem but small.

Third, Some of the Saints of God have not hesitated to think, that the torments of Purgatory are not inferior to those of Hell, only that those of Hell have no end, whereas those of Purgatory are but for a time.

Fourth, The following passages from the prophets, though addressed directly to the Jews, are applied, in their spiritual sense, to show the greatness of torments of Purgatory, "If the Lord shall wash away the filth of the daughters of Sion, by the spirit of judgment, and by the spirit of burning," Is. iv. 4. "And he shall sit refining and cleansing the silver, and he shall purify the Sons of Levi, and shall refine them as gold, and as silver, Mal. iii. 3.

"WHEN THE NIGHT COMETH NO MAN CAN WORK".

Q. Are the prayers, sacrifices, and other good works of the faithful upon earth of benefit to the souls in Purgatory, when offered to God for them?

A. Most undoubtedly they are of great service to them, both by easing their sufferings and shortening the time of their being there. The

THE SACRAMENT OF PENANCE 297

scripture expressly says, that "it is a holy and a wholesome thought to pray for the dead, that they be loosed from sins," 2 Macca. xii. In their situation they can do nothing for themselves but suffer till they have paid the last farthing. For, as our Savior assures us, when "the night of death cometh, no man can work," John ix. 4, and the Holy Ghost exhorts us to be diligent in doing all the good we can at present, for the same reason "whatsoever thy hand is able to do, do it earnestly; for neither work, nor reason, nor wisdom, nor knowledge shall be in hell, whither thou art hastening," Eccles. ix. 10, that is, in the regions below, in the state of the dead. But, though the souls in Purgatory can do nothing of themselves to ease or shorten their sufferings, yet such is the goodness of God, that in consideration of the union and charity which he so strictly requires among all the members of His Church, the body of Christ and of the Communion of Saints which he himself has established among them he is pleased to accept of the prayers, sacrifices, and good works of the faithful upon earth, when offered up by them for the souls departed; and, on that account, relieves their pains, and grants them a more speedy deliverance from them.

Q. Is it then a great charity to pray for the

souls in Purgatory?

A. It is certainly so; whether we consider *who they are, what they suffer, or how easily relived by us,* though they can do nothing for themselves.

BLESSED ARE THE MERCIFUL FOR THEY SHALL FIND MERCY.

Q. Is it very profitable to ourselves to pray for the souls in Purgatory?

A. It is one of the most profitable acts of mercy we can perform; for, *First,* "Blessed are the merciful, for they shall find mercy;" and, with the same measure that we mete to others, it shall be measured to us again." This is an established rule of the Divine Justice, consequently in being diligent in procuring relief to those who are gone before us, and are now in a state of purgation and suffering in the next life, is the most effectual means to move Almighty God to stir up others to bring the same relief to us, if we ever be so happy as to go to the same place; on the contrary, "judgment without mercy to him that shows no mercy," Jas. ii. 13.

Second, The souls in Purgatory are the beloved spouses of Jesus Christ, united to him by grace, and secure of their eternal salvation. Now, if Christ assures us that a cup of cold water given for his sake in this life, shall not want its reward, though the one to whom we give it may, perhaps, be one at enmity with Jesus Christ, or who will be lost for ever, and for ever separated from him; what reward will he give to those who, for his sake, contribute to do such a benefit to his beloved spouses in Purgatory, as to ease their dreadful torments, and procure them a more speedy admission to his Divine Presence?

Third, These holy souls themselves will sooner or later be admitted to the possession of God, to the clear and full enjoyment of the Divine Presence; what a happiness for us, if by our prayers, alms, sacrifices, and other good works, we have been instrumental in procuring them ease while they were in their state of purgation, and a more speedy admission to eternal bliss? May we not justly expect that their grateful hearts will not forget our services? will they not be so many steadfast friends to us in Heaven, and by their powerful prayers, obtain a blessing from God to our souls? Hence our Blessed Savior says, in the Gospel, " make to yourselves friends of the mammon of iniquity, that when ye shall fail, they may receive you into everlasting dwellings," Luke xvi. 9. And in this consists the communion we have with these blessed souls in Purgatory, included in that article of the Creed *the communion of saints;* which extends to all the members of the Church of Christ, whether they be as yet in this present life, or departed out of it to another; for we communicate to the souls in Purgatory the fruits of our prayers and good works offered up for them; and, in return, we receive, through the mercy of God, these precious rewards of our charity.

THE SOULS IN PURGATORY SHALL AT LAST BE SAVED.

Q. What instructions do we learn from this doctrine of Purgatory?

A. Chiefly these following: *First,* The strictness and severity of God's justice, which appears, in some respect, more formidable from Purgatory than even from Hell itself; for, in Hell, *whom does he punish?* His enemies, His rebellious creatures, obstinate, ungrateful, impenitent sinners, just objects of his aversion, wrath, and indignation; but in Purgatory, He punishes his beloved friends, the chaste spouses of His Son, the living members of Jesus Christ, the objects of His complacency and love. In Hell *how does he punish?* with torments the most dreadful, yea, more dreadful that can enter into the heart of man to conceive. In Purgatory he punishes with torments much of the same nature; for the souls there shall, indeed, at last, be saved, *yet so as by fire;* and, perhaps, little inferior in its intenseness, and differing from that of Hell only in its duration. In Hell *for what does he punish?* for mortal sin, the greatest and most atrocious outrage that can be done to his Divine Majesty; in Purgatory, he punishes only smaller sins, venial imperfections, human frailties. If, therefore, he punishes these venial imperfections in his own beloved friends in so severe a manner, how dreadful are his judgments? how severe his justice? how much to be dreaded and feared?

Second, Purgatory shows us, in the strongest colors, the great evil of venial sin; for God is a God of infinite justice, and therefore, can never punish any sin more than it deserves; he is also a God of infinite mercy, which inclines him to punish sin rather less than it deserves. If, therefore, a God of infinite justice punishes venial sin in so dreadful a manner in Purgatory, we must, of necessity, acknowledge, that venial sin most justly deserves that punishment; and if so, how great an evil it must be? how pernicious to those who are guilty of it?

WE MUST DISCHARGE THE DEBT WE OWE TO DIVINE JUSTICE.

Third, It also shows us the great advantage we may draw from the sufferings of this life, if borne in a penitential spirit; and from endeavoring by a truly penitential life of self-denial and mortification, to discharge the debt we owe to the Divine Justice, and by that means, "make agreement with our adversary while we are in the way." One great reason why souls go to Purgatory, is, because they have not satisfied the justice of God by their sufferings before they die; for this reason they must suffer in Purgatory till they have paid the last farthing. But such is the goodness of God, that he accepts the penitential works we do in this world, and the sufferings we bear in a penitential spirit here, as payment of that debt; and, as our sufferings here scarce deserve the name of sufferings, in comparison with the torments of Purgatory, this shows what a vast advantage we may draw from the afflictions of the present life, and how unreasonably we act by neglecting to make the proper use of them.

Fourth, We learn also from the same truth, how great esteem we ought to have for the indulgences which the Church grants us from time to time, and how careful and diligent we ought to be to use every opportunity of gaining them; if we are always properly disposed, and faithful in performing the conditions prescribed, they will undoubtedly be of the greatest benefit to our souls in discharging our heavy debt, either in whole, for what is past, if we be so happy as to gain a Plenary Indulgence, or at least to a considerable degree in proportion to our dispositions and diligence in doing our part.

In Loving Memory Of

Name	Date
St. Peter	
St. Andrew	
St. Jacob	
St. John	
St. Philip	
St. Barthelemeo (Nathaniel)	
St. Mathew	
St. Thomas	
St. Jacob s/o Halpai	
St. Simon the zealot	
St. Jude s/o Jacob	